SPEAK UP!

First published in 2020 by White Lion Publishing,
an imprint of The Quarto Group.
The Old Brewery, 6 Blundell Street
London, N7 9BH,
United Kingdom
T (0)20 7700 6700
www.QuartoKnows.com

A catalogue record for this book is available from the British Library.

ISBN 978 1 78131 950 5
Ebook ISBN 978 1 78131 951 2

10 9 8 7 6 5 4 3 2

Design by Isabel Eeles
Cover by Josse Pickard

Printed in Singapore

SPEAK UP!

· Adora Svitak ·

SPEECHES BY YOUNG PEOPLE TO EMPOWER & INSPIRE

· Illustrated by Camila Pinheiro ·

WHITE LION
PUBLISHING

Contents

Introduction

As a little girl, I drafted a handwritten speech with my sister called the 'Kids' Declaration of Independence from the Groans'. ('Groans' was our shorthand for grown-ups.) We had good reason to declare our independence: we thought there was something terribly overrated about adulthood. In childhood, when it snowed, my friends and I delighted; my dad, and many of his grown-up peers, would harrumph at the weather report emanating from the car radio and mutter about traffic. All too often, adults seemed harried, displeased, and joyless.

Society tells us that kids are selfish and impulsive, that our power and self-determination has to be limited for our own protection. As a child, I was tired of hearing about all the things I couldn't do because I wasn't 'mature' enough. If the state of our world was what 'maturity' had wrought, maybe we all needed to go about growing up a little differently. So, at the age of twelve, I asked an important question in my speech at the 2010 TED conference: 'What can adults learn from kids?' The answer is quite a lot.

This collection of speeches by extraordinary young people is testament to what can be achieved by the next generation. From climate change to transgender rights, these are children and young adults proving that, regardless of age, when we dare to care and speak out Groans in power take note, and can even learn a thing or two.

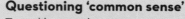

Questioning 'common sense'

Traits like impulsiveness, naivety and unguarded honesty are often panned as 'childish', but as we grow up it's easy to become desensitized to the way the world works. The Italian political philosopher Antonio Gramsci used 'common sense' to describe the myths, values, and visions of the world a society holds in common, pointing out that they often benefit those at the top the most. Why is it that we turn a blind eye to people sleeping on the street?

Why should anyone be ashamed of getting their period? Why do we discriminate against those we see as 'different'? 'That's just the way things are.'

But at the age of 10, 15 or 20, you haven't had as much time to absorb the confused 'common sense' of our society. So maybe, just maybe, the realities of injustice and poverty and environmental destruction still feel like horrifying surprises that have to be called out.

This naivety can produce the loudest of protestors. Take Swedish school girl Greta Thunberg as an example: aged 16, she lambasted world leaders at the United Nations for failing to address the climate crisis. Elijah Walters-Othman, a 17-year-old youth campaigner, spoke out in British Parliament to put a spotlight on educational inequality. In kindergarten, transgender rights advocate Jazz Jennings just wanted to be treated as the girl she knew she was inside, and didn't see why school administrators should think any differently.

For these brave young speakers, 'That's just the way things are' simply was not good enough. They believed in better and could not be deterred by towering obstacles and adults stubbornly bleating 'no'; they made it their mission to be heard and make a difference.

Stronger together

The 'Declaration of Independence from the Groans' ended up somewhere at the bottom of a recycling bin, but that moment foreshadowed my work to come, including organizing a conference by and for youth and speaking internationally about the importance of student input on educational reform. Gradually, I saw more and more students enter the public speaking and education space, and had the chance to meet inspiring student leaders like Tara Subramaniam, whose speech about her ground-breaking work with the non-profit organization Student Voice is included in this book.

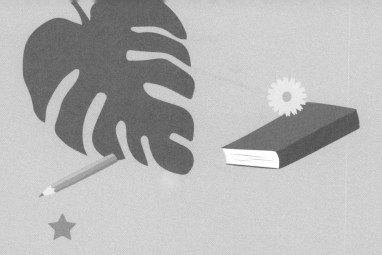

The process of researching took me to libraries and online archives, but most often down online rabbit-holes which began with a simple search query like 'Youth activists'. Little wonder that my online searches were the most fruitful: in our age of instant recording and uploading to the internet, speeches by young people may be more visible now than ever before. That's how I found Madison Kimrey. Despite not being old enough to cast a ballot herself, aged only 12, she spoke out against a state law that would make it harder for young people to register to vote.

My research helped me to understand the rich historical legacy of young people participating in political movements. From the tide of high school students in Johannesburg, South Africa who marched peacefully in June 1976 to protest apartheid, to the pro-democracy students in Hong Kong who held sit-in demonstrations during the 2014 Umbrella Movement.

From novice inventors to unlikely heroes, the stories of the talented figures featured in this collection teach us over and over again that we are all more powerful when research, fight, and we work together. We see team efforts like Madison Vorva and Rhiannon Tomtishen, the Girl Scouts fighting palm oil, or the Google Science Fair winners developing a powerful solution for global crop yields, Ciara Judge and Emer Hickey. Education advocate and Nobel laureate Malala Yousafzai has used her platform to amplify many other young people, like her friend, the Syrian activist Muzoon Almellehan. British student Amika George convinced over 200,000 signatories to support her petition to end 'period poverty', caused by lack of access to sanitary products. It was not only their curiosity, belief and dedication that sparked whole movements, but the help of friends and comrades worldwide.

Today, we live in a world of unprecedented connection, with more tools than ever to talk to people without regard to geographical distance. What kinds of communities could *you* build in pursuit of social change?

The bigger picture

Writing about 'passive youth' in her book, *The Feminine Mystique*, Betty Friedan said: 'There was literally nothing these kids felt strongly enough to die for, as there was nothing they actually did in which they felt really alive.' Growing up, I never wanted to be one of those kids, but it sometimes felt like it was hard not to be. In the face of daunting stakes, it takes bravery to pause, reflect, and worry about something larger than a score on a test or perfecting your resume.

But what if we put other priorities first? A desire to help those in need motivated Kenneth Shinozuka to begin designing smart products to improve safety for the elderly. Easton LaChappelle found the inspiration to develop low-cost and open-source prosthetics when he met a seven-year-old girl whose prosthetic arm had cost more than most Britons or Americans make in a year. Jack Andraka wanted to revolutionize tests for pancreatic cancer because of the loss of a close family friend, and Amanda Southworth turned her own struggles into the fuel for her mental health advocacy and an app to help others.

Instead of mindlessly competing with each other for entrance through a set of narrowing doors, these young people linked arms and demanded a world that works better for everyone. They teach us to question the status quo, develop new ideas and refuse to stand silently in the face of injustice.

I'm delighted to present a small sample of the many brilliant young minds worldwide who are proof that we have much to learn from the 42% of the world's population under the age of 25. Discover the determined voices that are changing our world, and the conversation. You'll find plenty who have worked together or inspired each other. I hope you'll be inspired too, and that this book might help you to find your own voice, spark your imagination and follow your dreams.

Joan of Arc

FRENCH HEROINE WHO FOUGHT DURING THE HUNDRED YEARS' WAR

As a teenage peasant girl living in medieval France, Joan of Arc began to hear voices she believed to be those of angels and of God. The voices instructed her to fight for the French king, Charles VII, during the Hundred Years' War. Adopting men's dress, she demanded to meet with military leaders such as the Duke of Lorraine and eventually Charles VII himself. Her persistence and conviction won her their trust. At the time, the French army was also in desperate straits. Perhaps the fact that so many other options had been exhausted and failed made Charles VII more open to the unorthodox choice of allowing a woman – and a young, poor one at that – to lead his troops. The gamble paid off: around the age of seventeen or eighteen, Joan led troops to victory at the Siege of Orleans.

When Joan's British adversaries captured her, they subjected her to relentless interrogations. They exhorted her to give up men's dress, emphasizing that she was only an ignorant girl who should trust the interpretations of men of the church rather than the voices she heard. She reiterated that she placed her faith in her voices, not her captors. In this excerpt from her trial for heresy, she speaks about hearing the voice for the first time. We see a picture of a young woman unbowed in her faith in God and unintimidated by powerful men, state power and the fatal price of her resistance.

Trial of Condemnation Interrogation Records

Rouen, France · 1431

If I were in a wood, I could easily hear the Voice which came to me ... I believe it was sent me from God. When I heard it for the third time, I recognised that it was the Voice of an Angel. This Voice has always guarded me well, and I have always understood it; it instructed me to be good and to go often to Church; it told me it was necessary for me to come into France ... It said to me: 'Go, raise the siege which is being made before the City of Orleans. Go!' ... And I replied that I was but a poor girl, who knew nothing of riding or fighting. I went to my uncle ... and said to him, 'I must go to Vaucouleurs.' He took me there. When I arrived, I recognised Robert de Baudricourt, although I had never seen him. I knew him, thanks to my Voice, which made me recognise him. I said to Robert, 'I must go into France!' Twice Robert refused to hear me, and repulsed me. The third time, he received me, and furnished me with men. The Duke of Lorraine gave orders that I should be taken to him. I went there. I told him that I wished to go into France ... I told him he was to send his son with me, together with some people to conduct me to France, and that I would pray to God for his health ... From Vaucouleurs I departed, dressed as a man, armed with a sword given me by Robert de Baudricourt, but without other arms ... Thenceforward I often heard my Voices.

Mario Savio

Berkeley, California, in the 1960s was a hotbed of political activity. The Free Speech Movement (FSM) began with a clash between progressive left-wing students and university administrators. The students, led by a group that included the civil rights advocate and activist Mario Savio, protested a school rule banning political content and organizing – including flyers and pamphlets – from entering the boundaries of campus. Mario Savio and others argued that this rule infringed on the students' rights to freedom of speech.

As administrators remained firm in their position, the students placed increasing pressure on the university: thousands of students stormed the campus's main administrative building, gathered in the main plaza and surrounded a police car so that it could not leave, and participated in sit-ins. Police conducted mass arrests but the movement continued for weeks, with protests and walkouts continuing until university officials backed down. Later, many of the students carried on their spirit of advocacy and community organizing, with movement building around pivotal issues such as protesting the Vietnam War.

The FSM was a defining moment in the history of student activism. Although college campuses would later become centres of protest, activism and civil disobedience, particularly around protesting American military actions overseas, the FSM was ground-breaking in its time and paved the way for future student political organizing and resistance.

The chancellor of the university eventually agreed to allow political activity on campus, thanks in no small part to the charisma and organizing of figures such as Mario. In his speech to fellow protesters gathered outside the university's administrative building, he criticized the market-oriented rhetoric of the university system's president and called for everyone to put their 'bodies upon the gears' of an unjust machine.

Sit-in Address on the Steps of Sproul Hall

University of California, Berkeley, California, USA · 1964

There are at least two ways in which sit-ins and civil disobedience ... can occur. One, a law exists ... which is totally unacceptable to people and they violate it again and again and again till it's rescinded ... Alright, but there's another way ... Sometimes, the form of the law is such as to render impossible its effective violation ... Sometimes, the grievances of people ... extend to more than just the law, extend to a whole mode of arbitrary power, a whole mode of arbitrary exercise of arbitrary power.

... And that's what we have here. We have an autocracy which runs this university. It's managed. We were told the following: If President Kerr actually tried to get something more liberal out of the Regents [university governing body] in his telephone conversation, why didn't he make some public statement to that effect? And the answer we received—from a well-meaning liberal —was the following: He said, 'Would you ever imagine the manager of a firm making a statement publicly in opposition to his Board of Directors?' That's the answer.

... Well I ask you to consider—if this is a firm, and if the Board of Regents are the Board of Directors, and if President Kerr in fact is the manager, then I tell you something—the faculty are a bunch of employees and we're the raw material! But we're a bunch of raw materials that ... don't mean to be made into any product! Don't mean to end up being bought by some clients of the University, be they the government, be they industry, be they organized labor, be they anyone! We're human beings!

... And that brings me to the second mode of civil disobedience. There's a time when the operation of the machine becomes so odious, makes you so sick at heart that you can't take part! You can't even passively take part! And you've got to put your bodies upon the gears and upon the wheels, upon the levers, upon all the apparatus—and you've got to make it stop! And you've got to indicate to the people who run it, to the people who own it—that unless you're free the machine will be prevented from working at all!

... That doesn't mean that you have to break anything. One thousand people sitting down some place, not letting anybody by, not [letting] anything happen, can stop any machine, including this machine! And it will stop!

And you've got to put your bodies upon the gears and upon the wheels, upon the levers, upon all the apparatus – and you've got to make it stop!

Mario Savio

Age 22

Severn Cullis-Suzuki

ENVIRONMENTAL ACTIVIST

When she was only twelve years old, Canadian climate change activist Severn Cullis-Suzuki delivered a brave message to an audience at the United Nations. In her speech, she said that many of the world's most privileged countries have failed to do their part in solving the climate crisis and providing assistance to the impoverished.

Now, more than two decades on from her 1992 speech, the recording of her talk still makes the rounds on social media as a viral video entitled 'The Girl Who Silenced the World for 5 Minutes'. Her message, which illustrates in bleak terms the consequences of failing to solve climate issues, has struck a chord with modern listeners. Her earnestness and hearkening back to adults' best intentions (e.g. what they teach their own children) raises a mirror to her audience's conscience and forces them to look it in the face.

Severn paid her way to the United Nations Earth Summit in Rio de Janeiro by raising money with other children – all students who had joined her Environmental Children's Organization (ECO). In one interview, Severn said that her father, the famed Canadian environmentalist David Suzuki, would try to give her and her fellow youth activists ten minutes of his speaking time when he was invited to conferences. She added, 'Because we were so young, what we had thought would be a barrier was actually the reason people paid attention.'

Her UN speech reminds all listeners, children and adults alike, that our inaction on climate issues is a profound indictment of our ability to live by our moral ideals. As an adult, Severn lives through the spirit of her 1992 talk: she continues to speak out for climate justice and advocate for world leaders to pay attention to the voices of youth.

Listen to the Children

United Nations Conference on Environment and Development (UNCED),

Rio de Janeiro, Brazil · 1992

Coming up here today, I have no hidden agenda. I am fighting for my future ... I am here to speak for all generations to come. I am here to speak on behalf of the starving children around the world whose cries go unheard. I am here to speak for the countless animals dying across this planet, because they have nowhere left to go. I am afraid to go out in the sun now, because of the holes in our ozone. I am afraid to breathe the air, because I don't know what chemicals are in it ...

Did you have to worry of these things when you were my age? All this is happening before our eyes and yet we act as if we have all the time we want and all the solutions ... You don't know how to fix the holes in our ozone layer. You don't know how to bring the salmon back up in a dead stream. You don't know how to bring back an animal now extinct. And you can't bring back the forests that once grew where there is now a desert. If you don't know how to fix it, please stop breaking it.

... Here, you may be delegates of your governments, business people, organizers, reporters, or politicians. But, really, you are mothers and fathers, sisters and brothers, aunts and uncles—and all of you are someone's child. I'm only a child, yet I know we are all part of a family—five billion strong; in fact 30 million species strong—and borders and governments will never change that. I'm only a child, yet I know we are all in this together and should act as one single world towards one single goal ...

In my country we make so much waste, we buy and throw away ... Yet Northern countries will not share with the needy. Even when we have more than enough we are afraid to share; we are afraid to let go of some of our wealth ...

Two days ago, here in Brazil, we were shocked when we spent time with some children living on the streets. This is what one child told us: 'I wish I was rich and if I were, I would give all the street children food, clothes, medicines, shelter, and love and affection.' If a child on the streets who has nothing is willing to share, why are we who have everything still so greedy? ...

In kindergarten, you teach us how to behave in the world. You teach us not to fight with others, to work things out, to respect others, to clean up our mess, not to hurt other creatures, to share, not be greedy. Then why do you go out and do the things you tell us not to do? ... My dad always says, 'You are what you do, not what you say.' Well, what you do makes me cry at night. You grown-ups say you love us. But I challenge you, please, make your actions reflect your words.

I have no hidden agenda. I am fighting for my future ...

_____

Severn Cullis-Suzuki

Age 12

Rhiannon Tomtishen
and Madison Vorva

ENVIRONMENTAL ACTIVISTS

When Girl Scouts Rhiannon Tomtishen and Madison Vorva were eleven years old, they set out to earn a Girl Scout Bronze Award. They took inspiration from their hero, the pre-eminent primatologist Dame Jane Goodall. Following in her footsteps, the pair decided to research an endangered great ape (orangutans rather than Goodall's chimpanzees).

Their research would instead take them down a rabbit hole of learning about the disastrous environmental effects of palm oil. They found that the cultivation of palm oil contributes to habitat destruction as vast swathes of the rainforest are chopped down to make room for palm oil plantations, driving out the native orangutans. This launched the girls on a multiyear campaign involving petition-writing, contacting the heads of companies, protesting outside the White House, media appearances, and speeches to get the

Girl Scouts and numerous other organizations to reconsider their use of the common ingredient.

The United Nations termed the two girls 'Forest Heroes' for their environmental work, and Rhiannon and Madison's campaign grew over the years, attracting thousands of signatures to their petition – including one from their hero, Jane Goodall. As a result of their work, organizations such as the food manufacturer Kellogg, as well as the Girl Scouts, authored palm oil policies.

They spoke passionately about their beliefs and their work at the National Bioneers Conference 2012, explaining how Girl Scout cookies began their quest to alert the world to the destructive nature of creating palm oil plantations.

We can dream in a way that is not limited by an adult's perspective.

Rhiannon Tomtishen and Madison Vorva

Age 16 and 17

The Fight Against Palm Oil

National Bioneers Conference, San Rafael, California, USA • 2012

MV: How many of you would think that Girl Scout cookies contain an ingredient that results in rainforest deforestation, the endangerment of thousands of species and contributes to human rights abuses? I didn't, until six years ago, when we ... decided to research the endangered orangutan. We discovered that their habitat in Indonesia and Malaysia has been cleared, in fact 40 million acres, for palm oil plantations.

RT: Believe it or not, palm oil is found in 50 per cent of the products on grocery store shelves: everything from candy bars to cosmetics ... We decided we weren't going to eat anything with palm oil ... When we realized Girl Scout cookies contained palm oil, it was so shocking for both of us. It's part of Girl Scout law to make the world a better place and to use resources wisely. To us, using deforestation-free palm oil seemed like the only, and the right, thing to do. As eleven-year-olds, we decided it would be our mission to bring this issue to the attention of the Girl Scout organization.

MV: We partnered with a variety of environmental and social organizations to reach a wider audience ... We designed easily accessible online campaigns, including a petition on change.org that gained 75,000 signatures ...

RT: In May 2011, after five years of campaigning, we were able to score a meeting with Girl Scouts executives in New York City ... and they announced a new palm oil policy, an important step in the right direction. It's the first policy in the organization's hundred-year history to have ever been driven directly by girls ...

MV: Most people would view our age as a disadvantage when trying to create change ... but because we are youth, we have the luxury of imagining a vision that appears irrational, and we can dream in a way that is not limited by an adult's perspective.

RT: We took one of our biggest weaknesses—our age—and turned it into our strength. There should be no limiting factor when it comes to changing the world.

Jack Andraka

INVENTOR AND RESEARCHER

After a close family friend died from pancreatic cancer, Jack Andraka began researching the disease. Discovering that it is often detected far too late for medical interventions to succeed, he decided to try building a solution. He went from 'not knowing what a pancreas was' to rocketing into the international spotlight at the age of fifteen for developing an inexpensive paper sensor for pancreatic cancer that won the top prize at the 2012 Intel Science Fair.

Growing up, we are used to a societal narrative that tells us we need certain qualifications in order to make a difference – that we need to talk a certain way, have years of experience or know the right people. Jack hopes his story of using open-access scientific research to innovate will inspire anyone who has worried that a lack of formal credentials is an insurmountable roadblock to conducting scientific research and development.

Jack is also contributing to greater inclusivity in science and technology by speaking publicly about being a gay scientist, declaring that Alan Turing was one of the few LGBTQ role models he knew of growing up and that he hopes to inspire others to pursue science. In his speech at the X Prize Visioneering Conference, an event for futurists and innovators, he told his story and announced his newest innovation, an inexpensive spectroscopy device. Recently, he has begun to advocate open access to scientific research, insisting that paywalls should not get in the way of the millions out there just like him.

Vision Talk X Prize Visioneering
Conference, California, USA · 2013

[When I] found out that a close family friend had just passed away from cancer, I had an idea. Maybe with the internet ... I could find out more about this mysterious assassin that had taken him ... What I found was that there was a very grim story when it came to cancer: 85 per cent of pancreatic cancers are diagnosed late, when someone has less than a two per cent chance of survival. Why are we so bad at detecting pancreatic cancer?

... After I learned this, I decided I was going to do something. Armed with my ninth grade biology and some Google papers, I went in with a broad expectation of revolutionizing cancer ... Ten months later, after emailing 300 professors, getting 299 rejections, spending seven months in the lab, blowing up my cells fifty times, I finally ended up with one small paper sensor that cost three cents and takes five minutes to run ... It can detect the cancer in the earliest stages ... so it could lift the survival rate of pancreatic cancer ...

However, there's a problem ... It's based on antibodies ... they can only target one protein. What we're going towards in the future of medicine is being able to look at all diseases ... Now I'm building something called a Raman spectrometer ... I have the luck of making things simple and inexpensive ... I made one the size of a sugar cube ...

Imagine this: I'm a fourteen-year-old when I came up with the idea for pancreatic cancer detection. I didn't know what a pancreas was ... But using just Google and Wikipedia, I found a new way to detect pancreatic cancer. So, if I could do that, just imagine what you could do.

Easton LaChappelle

INVENTOR

Easton LaChappelle launched his inventing career at the age of fourteen, when he began tinkering with a prototype robotic hand. In his 'No Time for School' speech in 2013, he explained how meeting a seven-year-old girl with one arm at a science fair in Colorado was an epiphany. She had one prosthetic arm which cost $80,000 and Easton realized that he could translate his work with robotic arms to disrupt the current prosthetics industry and to help people. By using 3D printing technologies and making his designs available open-source, he is able to make mind-operated prosthetic arms that are relatively inexpensive, lightweight, fast to produce and easy to maintain, revolutionizing the lives of many handicapped people. His work gained such wide recognition that he was invited to the White House, where he used his robot prosthetic to shake hands with President Obama.

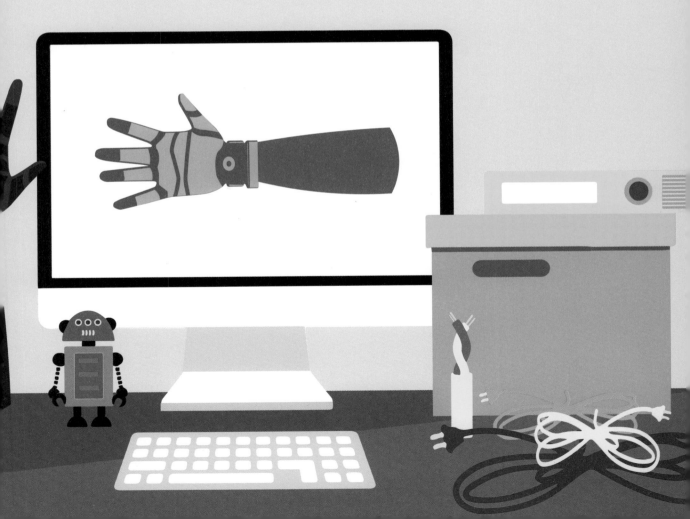

I could take what I'm already doing, transfer it directly to prosthetics and potentially make people's lives better.

Easton LaChappelle

Age 16

No Time for School

BIF-9 Collaborative Innovation Summit, Providence,

Rhode Island, USA · 2013

I had an idea when I was fourteen ... to create a robotic hand controlled by a wireless-controlled glove ... I turned to the internet as the main learning tool—teaching myself programming, electronics, different mechanics, CAD software, everything that would go into this project.

... The first prototype was really cool—it was a robotic hand with electrical tape and tubing as the fingers, and LEGO pieces as supports. That's just what I had laying around, and it worked really well ... When you put on the glove ... the robotic hand will wirelessly copy your movements; you could be anywhere in the world and control the hand accurately ... For bomb defusal, for the military ... they could put on this glove and it'd be as if they're out there. It does exactly what you do.

... Instantly, when I got into this, I wanted to make more, make cooler things. There was this new evolving technology called 3D printing ... I sent off all the designs [for the robotic hand] to this company in Colorado to have it 3D-printed and I got a quote of upwards of $500 just to print the hand. Being fourteen, I didn't have $500 to put into an idea ... I didn't know what to do after this. So I started networking. I had a friend working at MakerBot Industries, a private 3D-printing company ... and he threw it on one night and I just had to pay for shipping. This was the key that set this off. This newer hand has more functionality, it's a lot more practical than a hand with electrical tape all over it. It has individual joint control, an opposable thumb ...

When I was at a science fair in Colorado, I had the first generation of the arm there, and I was showing it to the public when a seven-year-old girl came up to me. She had a prosthetic limb from the elbow to the fingertip, with one motion (open-close) and one sensor. That alone was $80,000. That was the moment that really touched my heart, it was the a-ha moment—that I could take what I'm already doing, transfer it directly to prosthetics and potentially make people's lives better.

Kelvin Doe

INVENTOR

Growing up as the youngest of five children in a poor shanty town of Sierra Leone's capital, Freetown, Kelvin Doe did not have many opportunities to formally learn electrical engineering. He played among scrap electronics equipment that he found discarded around his neighbourhood, saving choice pieces to bring home and tinker with. His tinkering paid off: using old pieces from DVD players, he was able to build a generator to charge batteries, and a music and radio broadcasting set-up that inspired him to adopt the name 'DJ Focus'.

His resourcefulness attracted the attention of a visiting scholar from the Massachusetts Institute of Technology (MIT) named David Sengeh, who invited Kelvin to join a visiting delegation of inventors. At fifteen years old, Kelvin attracted media attention as the youngest visiting practitioner at MIT.

His story of innovation in the most unlikely of circumstances has captivated audiences around the United States, where he has received invitations to speak at conferences such as TEDxTeen. In his speech at Google Israel, he told his own story and encouraged members of the audience to encourage the creative passions of other young people like himself, no matter what their circumstances.

Moonshot Thinking

Google Israel, Tel Aviv, Israel · 2013

At the age of eleven, I started picking up scrap metal items on my way home ... My mother would wake up most nights to see our living room transformed into a small electrical scrapyard, and she would insist that I go back to bed ... With scrap, I could make things work, like my battery and FM radio station. I started fixing radios for people in my community for free. In places like my community in Sierra Leone, the most valuable asset in most households is the radio. The radio serves as a main source of news, music and family entertainment.

... I decided to turn to building my own circuit board, sound amplifier and a microphone receiver ... I called myself DJ Focus ... and started playing music for people in my community ... I loved listening to DJs on music stations ... and dreamed one day of being on the radio like them. [At the age of fourteen] it occurred to me that I could make my own radio station ... I spent many consecutive nights working on it ... I climbed on the roof, adjusted the antenna, and my FM radio station was on ...

I got into trouble when I discovered my broadcast signal was jamming that of a famous radio station in Sierra Leone. My mom ... told me to take my station off the air so I would not be arrested. Fortunately for me, I was able to change the frequency and still keep the station on air. The national television station in Sierra Leone heard about what I had done and put me on the air for a live demonstration ... Later, I became the youngest visiting practitioner at MIT ...

I urge you to look for young people's creative abilities and passion in all places, not just in places you might expect to find it. I ask you to support these young people, just as so many people have supported me.

Madison Kimrey

POLITICAL ACTIVIST

In a democratic society your vote is your voice. However, for many young people it is a right that feels inaccessible. The process of signing up to vote is not always as straightforward as it should be. In the United States, voters have to take the initiative to register to vote, and the process can be more difficult in states that do not prioritize increasing voter turnout. A particularly large problem is low voter turnout by young people. In response, one solution is pre-registration: making it possible for youth to register to vote in advance of their eighteenth birthdays so that they will be automatically added as soon as they turn eighteen.

Madison Kimrey's home state of North Carolina gave youth access to pre-registration. However, in 2013 her state's lawmakers passed a law taking away convenient access to pre-registration, meaning that young people would have to wait until turning eighteen to register to vote.

Although Madison was only twelve when she gave this talk – not yet old enough to vote herself – she identified this curtailment of opportunities to register as a threat to her and her peers' participation in democracy. Despite being called a 'prop' by her own governor, she stood strong in opposition to the new law and encouraged other young people to take an interest in political issues. In 2016, three years after Madison's speech, the youth of North Carolina won a political victory on preregistration thanks to a court ruling requiring the state to re-institute pre-registration.

Taking on North Carolina's Governor over Voting Rights

North Carolina, USA · 2013

We young people have a serious leadership problem here in North Carolina. We have leaders here in our state who have shown that not only do they want to reduce the amount of participation by young people in our government, they also want to dismiss and belittle our voices. Part of the new voter ID law that was passed by the North Carolina general assembly and signed by the governor eliminated the ability of sixteen- and seventeen-year-olds to pre-register to vote ...

I wanted to meet with our governor to discuss pre-registration but he called my request to meet ridiculous and called me a 'prop for liberal groups'. This is not leadership. I am not a prop. I am part of the new generation of suffragettes and I will not stand silent while laws are passed to reduce the amount of voter turnout by young people in my home state ...

I'm going to do everything I can to get the opportunities for North Carolina's teenagers to pre-register back by the time I turn sixteen in four years. But I can't do this alone. I need other young people to contact their lawmakers. I need other young people to talk to their friends and family about the issue. I need the adults who can vote to ask their elected representatives and candidates taking office how they plan to encourage young people to take an active part in our democracy. Young people, our state needs you. Our nation needs you ... Find the issues that are important to you and take action. We are the future of North Carolina and we deserve leadership that recognizes North Carolina's future and respects our ideas and our voices. The future of our state and our nation deserves no less than for us not to give up. Let's get out there and work.

Joseph Kim

NORTH KOREAN-AMERICAN HUMAN RIGHTS ACTIVIST

Joseph Kim grew up in utter deprivation, living in impoverished conditions during the North Korean famine of the mid-1990s. North Korea's isolation and secrecy make it impossible to know the precise number of casualties due to starvation, but estimates range from a few hundred thousand to over one million. Joseph's father was one of those casualties.

When Joseph was just sixteen years old, he made the decision to attempt an illegal – and highly dangerous – escape from the infamously oppressive Hermit Kingdom. If found by Chinese border guards, would-be escapees are typically turned back to North Korea, where they face death or imprisonment in vast detainment camps known for their cruelty. Joseph managed to evade detection while crossing the border.

From China, he travelled to the United States as a refugee, where he built a new life away from everything and everyone he had known. His experiences have made him a powerful advocate for human rights in North Korea and a supporter of US-based organizations that seek to aid refugees looking for a better life outside its borders. In his speech at the Ciudad de las Ideas (one of his many public speeches), Joseph spoke about his own story and how his journey to the US was made possible by the underground operations of the NGO (Non-Governmental Organisation) Liberty in North Korea (LiNK), which provided him with the shelter and resources needed to flee to the US.

In 2015, Joseph authored a memoir entitled *Under the Same Sky: From Starvation in North Korea to Salvation in America*. In the introduction, he wrote, 'The famine in North Korea killed hundreds of thousands of people. But the famine also did secret things ... Even if your body survived, you would find someday that your soul had been marked in ways you couldn't know until much later. That was true of many people I met in those times. And it was true of me.'

Joseph continues to use research and writing to help illuminate the issues of human rights and refugee resettlement. He works at the George W. Bush Presidential Center's Human Freedom Initiative, and has promoted assistance for refugees in the Center's journal of ideas: 'Protecting refugees in these situations is costly. But failing to save them is even more expensive. When international politics leaves them unattended or neglected, we lose part of our humanity and civilization takes a step backward.'

Hope is personal.
It is something no one
can give to you; you have
to make it yourself.
Don't try to find hope —
try to make your own.

———

Joseph Kim

Age 23

Speech at Ciudad de las Ideas

Ciudad de las Ideas, Puebla, Mexico • 2013

When I was young, I was just an ordinary boy in North Korea. I had a hard time waking up in the morning, spent almost all day acting out adventures of my favourite cartoon characters, climbing the trees, jumping down, thinking that I could fly one day. But when I was thirteen, everything changed. My father died of starvation. Soon after, my sister went to China to earn money. She promised me that she would return soon with my favourite food. And then my mum disappeared one day. Since then, I haven't seen them.

... I became an orphan, one of many homeless boys and girls in North Korea at that time ... I found myself on the street begging for food. I went up to the customers in the local market asking them, 'Can you please give me your leftover soup?' more than a thousand times in my head before I said it out loud ... I gave up living as a human; all I worried about was surviving ...

The train station where I used to come with excitement to visit my grandparents in another town became a place to rest for a long chilly night with an empty stomach. My first night ... I cried so much lying down on the corner of a wooden bench. The station reminded me of the past, the times I came here with my parents and my sister, waiting for the train to come ... What made me cry the most was not the hunger, pain or cold; it was the loneliness, the emptiness in my heart.

... I saw countless malnourished children lying on the dirt, agonised with hunger, waiting for their time to come. Once, I saw a five-year-old boy ...

repeating the same words over and over: 'Food. Food. Food.' The next day he began to call, 'Mum, Mum, where are you, Mum?' The next two days he just whispered so softly that I couldn't understand what he was trying to say. When he died, the police came and took away the corpse ...

When I could not fall asleep from bitter cold or hunger pains, I hoped that my sister would come back to wake me up the next morning with my favourite food. That hope kept me alive ...

After three years of waiting for my sister to return, I decided to go to China to look for her myself ... I knew the journey would be risky, but I would be risking my life either way: I could die of starvation like my father did ... or I could at least try for a better life by escaping to China ... I made it to China on February 15th, 2006. I thought things in China would be easier, since there was more food ... But I was always worried about being caught and sent back. By a miracle, some months later, I met an NGO called Liberty in North Korea, or LiNK. With their help, I was able to go to the United States as a North Korean refugee.

... My life in America was different. The nights became shorter and shorter. It was easier to sleep, because I had food, I had blankets, I had a place to sleep ...

Hope is personal. Hope is something no one can give to you; you have to make it yourself. Don't try to find hope – try to make your own hope ... Don't give up.

Melissa Shang

ADVOCATE FOR DISABILITY
RIGHTS AND REPRESENTATION

Have you ever felt invisible?

For Melissa Shang, invisibility comes from not seeing any characters like herself in books, movies or TV shows. As a young girl with muscular dystrophy, a disease that causes progressive muscle weakness and loss, she has to deal with both physical challenges and the general public's lack of awareness about what it is like to live with a disability.

Melissa wanted to change the narrative and show the world that girls with disabilities have stories worth telling as well. At the age of ten she started a petition to the American Girl doll company, asking them to make a doll with a disability. Her petition garnered over 150,000 signatures. Although the company did not release such a doll, Melissa did not give up, and used her newfound platform to continue advocating for others with disabilities. She co-authored a children's book with her older sister, *Mia Lee Is Wheeling Through Middle School*, featuring a main character in a wheelchair whose disability is visible but not defining. After all, as Melissa reminds us in her speech from the Day of the Girl at the United Nations, disabled girls 'are the same as other girls on the inside'.

Dreams of a Girl with a Disability

Day of the Girl, United Nations,
New York City, USA · 2014

Sometimes I feel that I'm invisible. I'm an eleven-year-old Chinese-American girl, and I've had Charcot-Marie-Tooth, a form of muscular dystrophy, for as long as I can remember. Being a disabled girl is hard, no matter where you live, even in the United States. Muscular dystrophy prevents me from activities like running and ice-skating and all the stuff that other girls take for granted. I'm often left out of activities. My fifth-grade teacher couldn't take me on a school field trip to a farm because the farm wasn't handicapped accessible ... I spend recess talking with friends at the edges of the playground while my classmates jump rope, play hopscotch or swing across the monkey bars. Even in the classroom, I can't take notes like other kids, but have to use special tools ...

People often forget that disabled girls have dreams too. We might be different from normal girls on the outside—we might be in a wheelchair like I am or have other difficulties that other girls don't have—but we are the same as other girls on the inside, with the same thoughts, feelings and dreams.

... When I watch movies and TV, it's like disabled girls are invisible. There are never stories about us. Being a disabled girl is hard, but even if we are weaker on the outside, disabled girls are stronger on the inside, because we face so many obstacles. I hope someday all disabled girls will have the chance to tell their stories and be treated just like everyone else.

Jazz Jennings

TRANSGENDER RIGHTS ADVOCATE

Jazz Jennings is a LGBTQ rights activist, YouTube and television star, and public speaker who shares her personal story around the world to convey a message of love, hope and acceptance for other transgender youth. Assigned male at birth, Jazz knew from a young age that she identified as a girl, and with her family fought for the chance to be recognized as her true self in school and on the sports field. They had to challenge the United States Soccer Federation so that she could play on girls' teams while growing up, and also had to deal with school administrators who did not fully understand or accept that a child in kindergarten could be sure of a gender identity different from the one they were assigned at birth.

Jazz is now featured in a reality show (*I Am Jazz*), the author of a memoir about her life and co-author of a children's book (*I Am Jazz*) about her childhood. She is also the co-founder of a foundation (TransKids Purple Rainbow Foundation) intended to help trans children. The organization sponsors events for transgender youth, provides scholarships to summer camps, donates funds to research and provides financial support to homeless trans youth and families.

In her speech at the HRC Foundation's Time to Thrive Conference, she highlighted the importance of supporting policies that allow children to express their gender identities freely, especially at school, and expressed gratitude that she is now surrounded by adults who create a safe environment for her to learn and grow.

I am proud of the way I am, and wish that all transgender kids could embrace their uniqueness like I do.

Jazz Jennings

Age 14

Jazz Jennings at the 2015 HRC Foundation's Time to Thrive Conference

Portland, Oregon, USA • 2015

I am a typical fourteen-year-old girl. I love to hang out with my friends, play soccer and tennis, draw and write stories, and most of all I love to binge-watch TV shows on my laptop. Oh, and I also just happen to be transgender. To be clear, that last point is not a negative. Being transgender makes me special and has helped to shape the person I am today. I am proud of the way I am, and I wish that all transgender kids could embrace their uniqueness like I do. I share my story so that my message of loving yourself and knowing that it's okay to be different can be spread everywhere.

When I was born, I was assigned male on my birth certificate. But from the moment I could express myself, I acted very feminine. I was drawn to anything sparkly, pretty and girlish ... I wanted to be exactly like my mom and my older sister ... You could always find me dolled up like a mermaid or princess, wearing ... beaded necklaces and those plastic high heels ... that cost a fortune at the Disney store ... When I was three years old, I called myself 'Sparkles' as a nickname ... It was at this time that I began insisting that I was a girl ...

In preschool, I met with a lot of opposition from the school administration ... Transgender pre-schoolers were unheard of. As kindergarten approached, my parents knew it would be harmful ... to force me to conform and start elementary school as a boy. In anticipation of resistance from the school administration ... my parents called a meeting with the principal months before the school year was set to begin ... [The principal] couldn't wrap her head around the idea of what she thought of as a little boy attending her school as a girl. She was adamantly opposed to me starting school as a girl ... and suggested I start instead with no pronouns ... After much pressure, she conceded to allowing me to use female pronouns ... The only area we couldn't get her to budge on were the dreaded bathrooms ... When I wasn't in my classroom, the school administration let me use the nurse's bathroom, which is where kids came in vomiting, or with bad cuts and bloody noses. I was terrified to use the infirmary restroom. As a result, I would hold my bladder and would often have accidents ...

My parents were busy fighting for my rights to play girls' travel soccer and decided ... to put the bathroom issue on hold for a few years ... Fortunately, by the time I was in fifth grade, we got a new principal and the school board passed a policy to protect the rights of all gender nonconforming students. I was happy to finally pee in peace. I'm happy to say that I'm now in middle school, and the administration is on board 100 per cent. My wonderful principal made it clear that I would always be treated like all the other girls ... I play on the girls' team in sports and I can wear what all the other girls wear ...

I consider myself a lucky kid now. There are adults in my school that I can turn to if I need something ... But back when I was younger, things could have been a lot better ... Every school district should have a policy protecting kids like me. Please keep in mind that close to 50 per cent of trans youth will attempt suicide by the time they are twenty-one. Each of you has the power to lower these statistics.

Malala Yousafzai

NOBEL PRIZE WINNER AND EDUCATION ADVOCATE

Malala Yousafzai is a Pakistani activist for peace and human rights, particularly passionate about equal access to education for women and girls. Although Malala had been an activist for years, writing for a BBC blog as early as 2009, it was in October 2012 that people around the world first learned her name. A Taliban gunman shot her on a school bus in a retaliatory attack over her public writings on education and life in Pakistan's Swat Valley during instability caused by clashes between the forces of the Taliban and the Pakistani military. Worldwide condemnation of the violent action followed and Malala was transferred to a UK hospital for medical care.

After making a full recovery, she founded a non-profit organization called the Malala Fund, which builds schools for girls and funds educational programmes through grants. Malala also authored a book entitled *I Am Malala*, and accepted the Nobel Peace Prize with co-recipient Kailash Satyarthi (a children's rights activist), becoming the youngest Nobel Laureate in history at the age of seventeen. She went on to deliver speeches around the world, including on numerous occasions at the UN; her speech in September 2015 focused on promises for children to live in a safe world where they can be educated in peace.

In 2017, Malala won a place at the University of Oxford to study politics, philosophy and economics. She is now internationally recognized as an advocate for education, refugees and women and girls; she influences world leaders, humanitarians, and 1.5 million Twitter followers.

Malala has used the high visibility of her position to draw global attention to those whose voices are often unheard: the millions of people around the world displaced due to conflict, some of whom she has met personally during her visits to refugee camps where the Malala Fund supports educational programmes. She co-authored a book entitled *We Are Displaced* about the plight of displaced people, adding in an interview with *The Guardian*, 'Sometimes we think about refugees as the victims. That they must have sad stories, and they are sad indeed, but they also show us how much courage they have and how brave they are.'

Speech at the United Nations General Assembly, New York

United Nations General Assembly, New York City, USA · 2015

Bismillah hir Rahman ir Rahim.

[In the name of God, the most beneficent, the most merciful.]

Before I start, may I ask for some quiet – please pay attention to what youth is asking here. Dear sisters and brothers, world leaders ... look up, because the future generation is raising their voice.

... Today, we are 193 young people representing billions more. Each lantern we hold represents the hope we have for our future because of the commitments you have made to the Global Goals.

... In my life, I have experienced terrorism, displacement and denial from education. And these are the tragedies that millions of children are still suffering.

... That shocking and heart-breaking image of [three-year-old] Aylan Kurdi lying dead on a seashore; the parents of the girls abducted by Boko Haram, with tears flooding from their eyes; and little children on the Syrian border with no home, no hope, force us to ask, 'How many more will we see killed, being rejected, neglected and being homeless in society? How many more?'

... The world needs a change. It cannot change itself. It's me, it's you, it's all of us who have to bring that change.

... Education is not a privilege. Education is a right. Education is peace.

... Dear world leaders, dear brothers and sisters, promise us, promise all children – children in Pakistan, in India, in Syria and across the world – promise them peace and promise them prosperity.

... Promise an education to my brave sister Salam and all refugee children, that wars cannot stop them from learning.

... Promise my sister Amina that our sisters abducted by Boko Haram will be brought back and that all girls will be able to study in safety.

Promise us that you will keep your commitments and invest in our future.

... Promise that every child will have the right to safe, free and quality primary and secondary education.

... This is the real investment the world needs and what world leaders must do.

... I am hopeful that we all, and the United Nations, will be united in the goal of education and peace. And that we will make this world not just a better place but the best place to live.

... Education is hope. Education is peace.

The world needs a change. It cannot change itself. It is me, it is you, it is all of us who have to bring that change.

———

Malala Yousafzai

Age 18

Patrick Kane

DISABILITY RIGHTS ADVOCATE

At nine months old, Patrick Kane almost died from a dangerous blood infection that caused major tissue damage and led to the amputation of his right leg below the knee, the fingers on his left hand, and two fingers on his right hand. He quickly had to adjust to a new life, wearing prosthetic limbs and dealing with other people's conceptions of what a disabled person could and could not do. However, as he wrote in *The Guardian*, his parents expected him to do everything other children could; this lack of externally imposed limitations meant that Patrick ran around and explored, just like his peers.

  Although the prostheses he used as a young child were somewhat primitive – frequently falling apart or needing to be adjusted for more comfortable wearing – he thought that they were good enough, until at the age of thirteen he became the youngest person to be fitted with a bionic arm, as he explained at his WIRED Next Generation speech in London in 2015. That experience changed his expectations for prostheses, as well as his ideas about what 'disability' might mean in the twenty-first century. With so many technological innovations at our fingertips, Patrick argues, our old ideas of what people with disabilities can do simply do not hold true anymore.

Why Technology Could End the Concept of Disability

WIRED Next Generation, London, UK · 2015

I believe [the word 'disability'] is becoming offensive to those who it is no longer able to describe ... This word makes assumptions about my own ability and the abilities of others, and more offensive still is that this word will prevent certain people from doing the things they are able to do because this word tells them they cannot ...

The reason why I think this word is going out of use is because technology is bridging the gap between disability and ability ... Blind people seeing, athletes running without legs and paraplegic people learning to walk again sounds like make-believe, and fifty years ago it definitely would have been. However, we are now at a crossroads where technology has the potential to overcome even human limbs ... Technology for me has been a huge part of my life. I learned to walk aged seventeen months on a prosthetic limb. Since I was born the Paralympic sprint time has decreased 3.2 per cent. It's taken able-bodied people forty-one years to achieve the same decrease ...

I'm incredibly lucky for so many reasons: first of all, I was born in London, a city which celebrates diversity and disability ... also I'm fortunate that I was born into a family that could afford the advanced prostheses I needed from a young age ... The fact that the government is not willing to pay for advanced prostheses that truly have the power to transform people's lives is upsetting to say the least.

... In summary, society uses a term which is no longer fit for its purpose. I don't see how we can continue using a word when it simply doesn't apply to everyone. I think it's damaging, and we need a new one. The real question is, what will it be?

Emer Hickey and Ciara Judge

SCIENTISTS

Emer Hickey and Ciara Judge are scientists who gained international acclaim for research with potentially expansive ramifications for world hunger and agricultural output. Both from Cork, Ireland, they started their research when they were just fourteen years old, after Emer found some bacteria on the roots of a plant while gardening and brought it to her science teacher. Once they had learned more about the bacteria, the team became interested in its potential to induce higher crop yields on other plants. Their work continued over the course of three years, taking over Ciara's guest room and then 'the kitchen, sitting room, conservatory and garden', testing over 14,000 seeds.

When they found that the rhizobia bacteria could increase some crop yields as much as 74 per cent, they decided they had found something worth amplifying to a larger audience and entered their research into several science fairs. Emer, Ciara and their teammate Sophie Healy-Thow went on to win several science fairs, including the European Union Contest for Young Scientists (where they were selected out of thousands of entries from over ninety countries), the BT Young Scientist and Technology Exhibition, and the Google Science Fair. The Google Science Fair prize included a National Geographic trip to the Galapagos Islands, a $25,000 scholarship and $50,000 grant towards their research project, and astronaut training with Virgin Galactic.

TIME magazine listed them in their Most Influential Teens in the World in 2014, alongside a flurry of positive media coverage from around the world. Emer and Ciara co-direct a research company called Germinaid Innovations that they launched in 2015, devoted to further work on agricultural solutions. They also support a team at the teen-run, entrepreneurship-supporting non-profit organization Project Zilkr. They believe strongly in the power of other young people to make change, and as they emphasized in their Start Now speech in 2015, their story is not unique and anyone with an idea can make a difference.

People think you have to be some sort of genius to carry out a project like this. You don't.

_____

Emer Hickey and Ciara Judge

Age 18

Start Now

WIRED Next Generation, London, UK · 2015

EH: Our whole story began when I was gardening with my mum ... We pulled peas up, and we found these ugly wart-like root-y things on them ... After doing a bit of research, we found that the bacteria called rhizobia lives within these nodules ... We decided that because of this bacteria we had just found out about, we were going to try and basically solve world hunger. That was what we wanted to do at fourteen.

CJ: We didn't have access to a lab or anything fancy, so we began by creating our own homemade lab in my spare bedroom at home ... building all the equipment we needed ... We also had to go out and learn a lot about working with bacteria that we hadn't covered in school yet. So we were exposed to a new side of science that we had never seen before. One that was outside the textbook.

EH: We'd get trays and lay out seeds all individually, and then we'd get the pipette and put an exact amount of bacteria solution on them. But the fun part was that every six hours we'd then have to look at these seeds and inspect each one individually for like a tiny little root. So we had to do this [every] six hours, that meant we might look at over a thousand seeds at 12 o'clock at night, which if we were lucky would take two hours, and then get back up again at 6am to do it all over again, for two weeks.

CJ: After we had experimented on more than 10,000 seeds, we analysed our results, and we found that we had actually managed to increase the speed of germination by 50 per cent and increased the craft productivity by up to 74 per cent. Obviously, this has quite large implications for the food crisis, and we were absolutely over the moon ...

EH: People think you have to be some sort of genius to carry out a project like this. You don't. We are far from that; we are not near that at all. It quite simply was a mix of hard work, passion and honestly a lot of luck. We happened to find out about a bacteria out of all the millions of bacteria, and then happened to put it on crops that it would work on. It was really luck. And what we discovered while doing this three-year-long project, is that it's actually easy in many ways to carry out anything really, once you're passionate about it. But it doesn't come without its many, many difficulties ...

CJ: If you're thinking of starting a project or an organisation or even a business, don't get overwhelmed by the mountain of work that'll be ahead of you because there will be a mountain of work ahead of you ... but just break it down into stages ... It takes hundreds of nights to become an 'overnight success' ... We just took the attitude that even if [this project] didn't work, at least we would know for sure and the rest of the world would know for sure. We would have proved something even if it wasn't exactly what we set out to prove. We would've done our bit and we would've contributed to the knowledge base of the world. And no matter what anyone tells you, that's something to be proud of ... Ordinary young people can make a massive, monumental difference to the world that we live in today.

Raymond Wang

INVENTOR

Between apocalyptic pandemic movies and germophobes' advice columns about which seat to pick to avoid catching colds, the aeroplane has been firmly established as a site of disease transmission in the popular imagination. However, Canadian inventor Raymond Wang was not content to let things stay that way. At the age of seventeen, as an eleventh-grader at St George's School in Vancouver, he started reading about the Ebola outbreak. Disturbed by the way in which conventional airflow in planes spreads pathogens among passengers, he began brainstorming new design interventions that could improve the chances of halting disease transmission in its tracks.

Using computer models that simulated the pathways of air in plane cabins, Raymond tested different inventions until he found one that worked. He called it the 'global inlet director', and it worked by adding a miniature fan to give every passenger a breathing zone of their own instead of recirculating the same air others had breathed – or sneezed or coughed into – everywhere else in the cabin. Raymond described this process and his invention in detail in his speech at the 2015 Ciudad de las Ideas.

That invention led to him winning the Gordon E. Moore award for Top Project in Intel's prestigious International Science and Engineering Fair, with a $75,000 prize. He received Canada's 20 Under 20 award and went on to attend Harvard University in Boston. Raymond's inventions have not been limited to smarter airflow on aeroplanes; his deep passion for sustainability has led him to also work on a Weather Harvester (a piezoelectric roof intended to store energy from weather), a Smart Knee Assistant (dynamically adapting knee support) and a Sustainable Smart Sanitizer (a treatment system powered by light that could deodorize and sanitize outdoor garbage bins). Raymond also founded a non-profit organization called Sustainable Youth Canada, devoted to empowering students around the nation to become climate leaders.

Speech at Ciudad de las Ideas

Ciudad de las Ideas, Puebla, Mexico · 2015

Right now I want you all to take a moment and imagine you're sitting inside this plane. Next to you are over 200 people, and you're about to spend the next ten hours of your life packed inside this metal tube to fly halfway across the world. What would happen if someone were to actually sneeze?

Hopefully not much, but there's actually a variety of diseases that could be transmitted within just that one sneeze. Influenza, SARS, and the list goes on and on. And with more than three billion passengers traveling in aircrafts every year, this can be a serious issue. A person with H1N1 managed to get on a flight and infect seventeen other passengers. A passenger flying on a three hour flight managed to infect twenty-two other passengers with SARS. It's very difficult to figure out whether a passenger has a disease in the first place, and to prevent them from getting on the plane, because there's this period of latency during which the passenger can have the disease but not exhibit any symptoms.

I thought, okay, there are these air filters that are already on planes. They're super efficient. They limit up to 99.9 per cent of pathogens. But your air filter's no good if the air doesn't pass through it. [In] the traditional cabin as it stands today, we get this huge mixing pattern that happens inside the airplane. When someone breathes out something that air actually gets passed around in cycles multiple times before it actually has a chance to go out into the air filters for filtration.

I thought this was a pretty big problem. How can we take a look at that sort of issue? First thing that came to mind was I don't have enough money to rent a plane and do all that sort of testing, but it turns out that there's a better alternative. I could build a computer instead! In the industry, this is what's known as using computational fluid dynamic software. And with this, we've actually gotten so good that the results that we get from this simulation are several times higher in resolution than what we'd get with actually going out and physically measuring airflow inside the cabin.

I went in and tested more than thirty-two different scenarios, making tiny tweaks to the cabin so that we're able to change the airflow pattern, and what I finally came up with was my patent pending 'global inlet director.' It's able to reduce pathogen transmission by about fifty-five times, and improve fresh air inhalation for the passengers by about 190 per cent. We leverage these existing cabin surfaces already in the planes. You'd take my innovation and install it, put a couple of screws in it, and overnight, you're good to go. It costs less than $1000 to manufacture for the entire cabin. And when we take a look at the improved cabin, the results are astounding.

Fundamentally anything just starts with an idea. For me it started with hearing about the news about the Ebola outbreak back in December, and from that, it's just being able to put this into action. You don't have to have a PhD to be able to tackle real issues. You don't even have to have a university degree. As human beings, we have been gifted with the fantastic ability to be able to create, and to be able to facilitate change. When we truly get together and when all of us here in this room and beyond commit to taking action, we can really improve the world for the better.

As human beings, we have been gifted with the fantastic ability to be able to create, and to be able to facilitate change.

Raymond Wang

Age 17

Megan Grassell

ENTREPRENEUR AND
CLOTHING DESIGNER

Megan Grassell was helping her little sister find her first bra when she had a startling realization: young women had nowhere to turn for age-appropriate choices in stores that offered nothing but hyper-sexualized bra options.

Instead of shrugging her shoulders at the status quo, Megan decided to do something. Despite being a self-described 'insecure seventeen-year-old girl' in her penultimate year of high school, she decided to take on the challenge of starting her own clothing line to provide better bras for girls like her sister.

In 2014, Megan raised over $40,000 on the crowdfunding platform Kickstarter to manufacture the bras. The company, which she named Yellowberry, became a runaway success, tapping into a market of parents who wanted better, less sexualized options for their young daughters' first bras. Since then, Megan has been named on the *TIME* magazine 25 Most Influential Teens list, as well as Yahoo's 24 Millennials to Watch and Forbes' 30 Under 30. Since its humble beginnings in Megan's home, Yellowberry has expanded to two offices.

Megan said in an interview with Forbes, 'My advice to pre-teen girls is to stand up straight and know exactly how smart, talented and awesome you are because that is the truth. Own it.' In her speech to the students of St Catherine's School, a girls' school in Richmond, Virginia, she encouraged audience members to innovate fearlessly when they see problems with the way things are.

Speech at St Catherine's School

St Catherine's School, Richmond, Virginia, USA · 2015

I took my younger sister shopping to buy her very first bra when she was thirteen years old ... I remember being so appalled that everything was super-sexualized. I had this vivid memory of her walking out of the dressing room in this padded, push-up leopard-print number and I just wanted to cover her up ... There was nothing available for her that was more age-appropriate, so I had this epiphany: if no one else was going to make bras specifically for girls, then I was going to find a way to make it myself ...

I Googled where to get fabric and sourced things from random different locations, took them in a basket to a seamstress in Jackson (which is where I'm from), and asked, 'Can you make a bra for me?' She said, 'Do you have a pattern?' I said 'yes' ... I had a hand sketch of a bra that looked like it had been done by a third grader. She just kind of laughed at me, and it was the first of many times I realized how much I didn't know ...

As I worked with the seamstress, trying on bras with my sister and her friends to see what they liked and didn't like, I also reached out to a lot of people in my community doing work around apparel or business ... Although I found some great advice and great mentors along the way, I also heard a lot of 'Honey, I think you should just finish high school before you try to revolutionize the bra industry.' But what stuck with me was when someone told me, 'This is just the way things are, sex sells, have you heard of Victoria's Secret?' If someone ever tells you 'this is just the way things are', that should spark something: that you can do it better. Because that's what innovation is, taking what you have right now and improving it, doing something better and progressing.

Kenneth Shinozuka

DESIGNER AND INVENTOR

Kenneth Shinozuka's inventive spirit stems from seeing problems faced by real people in his life. At the age of six, a family friend's fall in a bathroom led Kenneth to design a motion detection system for bathrooms that would send an alert to his wristwatch in case someone fell on the bathroom floor; although he did not turn his design into a prototype, it foreshadowed his future love of tinkering to produce health and safety solutions. When he was a young child, he saw his grandfather begin to lose the ability to take care of himself as Alzheimer's took its toll. One particularly worrying consequence of the disease's advance was that his grandfather would wander out of bed in the middle of the night, then not know where he was or how to get home. This meant sleepless nights for relatives who were caretaking, leading Kenneth – then fourteen years old – to create a sock sensor that would alert the carer when the person wearing the sensor got out of bed in the middle of the night.

Because of that invention, Kenneth garnered attention from numerous news outlets as well as the Google Science Fair; he also won the $50,000 *Scientific American* Science in Action Award and spoke at the TED conference in 2017. He runs SafeWander, a company which produces and distributes his invention.

In his speech at the Ideagen EU 2030 Leadership Summit, Kenneth accepted an award for the world-changing product, while demurring that he did not necessarily think his invention met the qualification for 'world-changing'. He asked what we mean when we say 'changing the world', suggesting that perhaps our grand visions belie the smaller-scale moments that add up to make world-changing actions possible.

My Simple Invention to Keep My Grandfather Safe

Ideagen EU Leadership 2030 Summit, New York, USA • 2015

'Changing the world.' What does that mean? ... When I think about changing the world, three things come to mind: first, ending poverty; second, forging international peace; and third, expanding education. Lots of big, giant ideas ...

But what often gets lost in that conversation is that changing the world can start from just one very small event in time, and one person. For me, my entire journey started with my grandfather. Growing up, my grandfather and I were very close ... When I was four years old, the two of us were walking in the park in Japan, singing our favorite songs to each other, and at one point his face suddenly went completely blank. And I knew he was lost. I was only four years old, so I didn't understand what was going on but I knew that he didn't remember the way to get back home ... The sixty minutes that it took my mom to find us was the scariest hour that I'd ever spent in my entire life. That one moment in time that he stopped singing turned out to mark the first sign of my grandfather's Alzheimer's disease.

Over the years his condition got worse and worse, and he started wandering out of bed at night frequently ... eventually at least once every night. My aunt had to stay awake all night to keep an eye on him, and even then sometimes failed to catch him leaving the bed ... I became very concerned about my aunt's wellbeing, as well as my grandfather's safety. One night ... on night watch for Grandpa ... I remember seeing him stepping

out of the bed, and the moment his foot landed on the floor, I had the sort of eureka moment, I saw the solution to my family's problems. I thought, why don't I put a pressure sensor under the heel of my grandfather's foot? As soon as he steps onto the floor, the pressure sensor will detect the increasing pressure and send an alert to my aunt's Smartphone, waking her up ...

There were so many challenges involved, but what was really rewarding at the end of the experience was one moment, a singular moment, when I had finished my prototype, integrated all these components together and decided to test it on my grandfather for the first time. I remember in the middle of the night we were all trying to figure out if this sensor would work. My grandfather stepped out of the bed, and we heard this faint alert beeping out. We knew the sensor was working ...

I felt in that moment not only that technology could change lives for the better, but the fact that my sensor could bring my entire family peace of mind. Just that one moment made me feel like the entire experience was very rewarding ... I pursued the idea ... and am starting to ship out the sensors today ... These big moments that define us and define 'changing the world' ... are all actually, if you think about it, really small; they start from one sliver of the vast continuum of time ... and one person in the giant pool of people we call our collective humanity. For me, it all started with one person getting lost ... These small moments define us.

Changing the world can start from just one very small event in time, and one person.

———————

Kenneth Shinozuka

Age 17

Tara Subramaniam

EDUCATION REFORM ADVOCATE

Tara Subramaniam is co-founder of the student-led non-profit organization Student Voice, which advocates for students to have more decision-making power within their schools. When she was still in high school, she joined other students who were organizing a weekly Twitter chat (a scheduled conversation on Twitter using a central hashtag) with the hashtag #StuVoice. The Student Voice discussion eventually grew to become one of Twitter's most popular education chats, with over 5 million views and even an appearance by US Secretary of Education, Arne Duncan.

Tara and her co-founders seized on the momentum created by that Twitter chat to start an organization that could hold listening sessions, publicize the demands of students and elevate students to positions on advisory boards and speaking roles in education conferences. The organization also wanted to set out a series of basic rights for students, leading them to draft a Student Bill of Rights to be a guiding document for their campaigning and advocacy in schools. Later, the organization undertook a national tour to visit all kinds of schools – including those that

suffered from incredible deprivation – and hear first-hand the experiences of students.

After Tara graduated from high school and went to Georgetown University, she led Student Voice to even more ambitious goals, as it garnered recognition in national news, started chapters in schools around the country and created resources to empower students to participate in driving change to local legislation. The organization promotes investigative journalism by students about the conditions of American schools through the Student Voice Journalism Fellowship, which has promoted journalism about topics ranging from inequitable access to arts education in public versus private schools to sexism in high school sports.

Tara's work as co-founder and later an executive director of Student Voice included evangelizing the work of the non-profit, not only to fellow students but also to movers and shakers in offices of power. She spoke about Student Voice's work at the White House's summit on the future of education in 2016.

Speech at the White House Next Gen Summit

White House Next Gen Summit, Washington, D.C., USA • 2016

During the summer before my sophomore year of high school, I, along with three college students, co-founded Student Voice, a student-run non-profit founded to inspire and empower students to take charge of their education. We are the only student-led organization to integrate student voices into the global education narrative and our efforts are strengthening the student movement for equitable schools.

... Two years ago, we launched a program called the Student Bill of Rights, which consists of twelve rights that, after consulting with students across the nation, we have identified as pillars of a quality education and positive school experience for an American student. The Bill of Rights is intended to serve as a framework for students to identify areas in which their schools are excelling and pinpoint where they could use help.

To further build upon our work with the Student Bill of Rights, we went into schools as part of our National Tour. The tour has opened my eyes [to] – and hopefully illustrated to those who follow our work—the startling disparity within the US education system.

On one hand, our National Field Director, Andrew Brennan, spent time in South Carolina's Corridor of Shame, which encompasses 132,000 students from thirty-six public school districts, some of which are so low on funds that students don't go to class—not because they don't want to, but because their teachers are paid so little it's not worth showing up to teach. On the other hand, a week later, our team was in sunny San Diego at High Tech High, where students are required to intern [in] their junior year. In both cases, students aren't going to class in a traditional manner, but for vastly different reasons.

... We must keep fighting for a positive school climate and for a modern education system until areas such as the Corridor of Shame receive the help, funds and motivation they need to look more like High Tech High and until all students can experience at least a portion of the support I had in high school.

We must keep fighting for a positive school climate and for a modern education system.

_____

Tara Subramaniam

Age 19

Joshua Browder

ENTREPRENEUR

Joshua Browder is a British-American entrepreneur who put the coding skills he taught himself at the age of twelve to good use when he developed the idea for the legal chatbot DoNotPay. In his 2016 speech he pointed out that his motivation emerged from a personal experience with parking tickets. He realized that he could turn his frustration into a productive way to help others dealing with similarly routine, yet irritating, interactions with the government – situations where a lawyer's assistance would be helpful and require only simple work but might also be prohibitively expensive. Joshua saw the potential to save people money and provide much-needed legal help by offering automated advice in response to common legal questions.

DoNotPay quickly became popular, with over 86,000 people using the chatbot. Joshua saw that the automation of legal help could have ramifications in areas beyond parking tickets. After seeing evidence of the chatbot's success in that area, he turned his attention to requesting compensation from airlines for delayed and cancelled flights. He was named one of the Forbes 30 Under 30 in 2016. In 2019 he launched a new app, Free Trial Surfing, intended to help people cancel free trials before inadvertently getting charged for goods or services they do not want or need at the end of the trial period.

Will Bots Replace Lawyers?

O'Reilly Next: Economy, San Francisco, California, USA · 2016

When I turned eighteen ... I got a large number of parking tickets. After about the fourth ticket, my parents were fed up. They told me I was on my own, and I had to pay for my own fines. But the problem was, I couldn't afford a lawyer or to pay the fines, so I had to figure out ways to get the tickets dismissed. I trawled through hundreds of pages of obscure government documents looking for the top reasons why these parking tickets should be cancelled. After some initial success, it wasn't long before all my family and friends were asking for my help.

... But it quickly became obvious that instead of helping everyone individually, I should create some sort of automated system to help people en masse. When I spoke to some lawyers in London about what they thought about the idea of a lawyer robot, some were more polite than others, but every single one said it was silly and would never work.

... But, thinking it would be a cool side project, I decided to create it anyway, and name the bot DoNotPay. It first asks the user a few questions about their parking ticket to find out the legal defence, such as a parking bay that is too small. It then asks to find out the details and then places these details in a legally sound document which can be sent directly to the government. Now, when I created this, it was really just to impress a few friends and I could never have imagined that just six months later DoNotPay would take the legal world by storm. In just under a year, it has successfully appealed over 180,000 parking tickets, saving motorists an estimated $5 million ... All of this made me realise that the idea of using bots to help people with automated legal issues is bigger than just parking tickets.

Krtin Nithiyanandam

SCIENTIST AND INVENTOR

Krtin Nithiyanandam's interest in science and research grew during a time when an injury kept him from playing sports; he devoted his newfound free time to independent research projects. One such project involved a diagnostic test for early-onset Alzheimer's disease. At the age of fifteen he entered the test into the 2015 Google Science Fair, where he ultimately won $25,000 for his innovation.

Around 50 million people worldwide are diagnosed with dementia; researchers believe Alzheimer's disease may make up 60 to 70 per cent of those cases. The prospect of memory loss that can affect one's ability to carry out basic tasks, live independently or even remember loved ones is terrifying, made even more frightening by a lack of treatment options. Alzheimer's is notoriously hard to detect for the same reason it is hard to treat. This is because of the blood-brain barrier, a semi-permeable barrier that

separates the brain from foreign substances and hormones and neurotransmitters in the rest of the body. Krtin developed a novel antibody complex that could bind to some of the most neurotoxic family of proteins associated with the onset of Alzheimer's, working out a way for it to cross the blood-brain barrier and be used in diagnosis of the disease.

Because of his work, *The Observer* named Krtin a 'Rising Star in Science', *TIME* magazine listed him as one of their 30 Most Influential Teens of 2017, and he received invitations to speak publicly about his research at venues such as the Royal Society of Medicine. At the age of sixteen, Krtin delivered a speech at the WIRED Next Generation conference discussing his research story, encouraging other young people to share their ideas with the world.

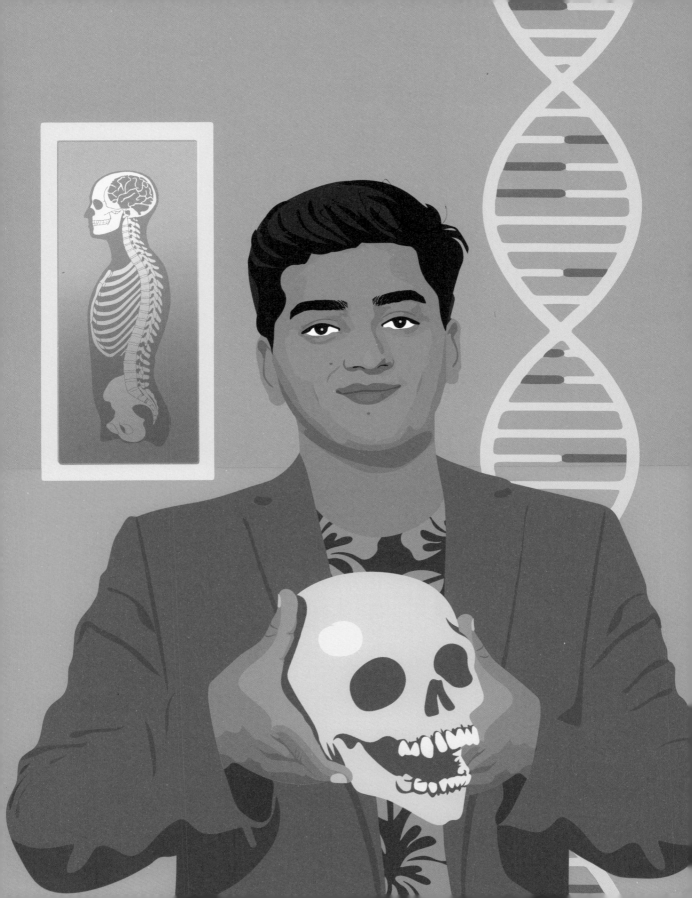

Science Isn't About Your Age, It's About Ideas

WIRED Next Generation, London, UK · 2016

I only got into research a few years ago, when I fractured my pelvis ... [Before] I used to play squash three or four days a week, and it was frustrating that I couldn't play anymore, but it did mean that with all this free time I could explore things I didn't have the opportunity to do so before. Science and research was one of those things.

... My first ever research project was on chelation therapy – it's used to treat metal poisoning, but it has a lot of side effects, which stops it from being used to treat other diseases. My first project was really straightforward – why chelating agents were causing these side effects, in the hopes of letting researchers develop better chelating agents that could be used to treat other diseases like Alzheimer's disease and cancer ...

I wanted to explore Alzheimer's disease next ... Alzheimer's disease affects over 47 million people worldwide and it cost society US$604 billion in 2010. This disease is notorious for the fact that there exists no drug to stop or slow down the progression of this disease, and only 45 per cent of patients receive a diagnosis in their lifetime. The other 55 per cent are post-mortem, or the diagnosis never happens. An early diagnosis is essential to ensure that the patient has a better prognosis.

I wanted to find a way to diagnose the disease earlier. I looked at a family of proteins called the amyloid beta family ... [Specifically] oligomers, present in significantly higher concentrations in the brains of Alzheimer's patients. We believe them to be the most toxic form of amyloid beta, but they're also present up to a decade before symptoms first start to show. So if you're targeting this protein, you have a massive head start in ensuring the patient gets a proper diagnosis, and the prognosis is favourable ... I was able to design an antibody ... that was more specific than existing antibodies ... Antibodies are far too big to cross the blood-brain barrier. To overcome this I use a method called receptor mediated transcytosis ... using that, the antibody complex is able to enter the brain ...

What was most frustrating about the research wasn't the theory or the actual experimentation process, it was getting started. I emailed fifty-four different labs before I got one positive response, and that was three months after I first emailed them ... I can see where they're coming from; getting an email from a fifteen-year-old asking for access to toxic chemicals and expensive equipment does tend to make people uneasy ... But science, I think, is not about how old you are – it's about having ideas. As long as you have an idea, you have something you can work on ... There are 1.2 billion teenagers in the world between the ages of ten to nineteen, that's 1.2 billion minds full of potential and world-changing ideas. A lot of ideas remain just that – ideas – because most of the time we don't do anything to pursue them, but in a world that is so connected and inter-dependent we can't give the excuse anymore that we don't have the resources to do so, we just have to go out there and get them.

A lot of ideas remain just that – ideas – because most of the time we don't do anything to pursue them.

———————————

Krtin Nithiyanandam

Age 16

Ishita Katyal

YOUTH ADVOCATE

Ishita Katyal from Pune, India, believes that age should not be a restriction that keeps anyone from achieving their dreams. She exhorts adult audiences to shift from asking young people, 'What do you want to be when you grow up?' to asking what they can do right now and to supporting their aspirations.

When she was just aged eight, she wrote a children's book, *Simran's Diary*, featuring an eight-year-old girl as its main character and chronicling her happy, sad and funny moments. At the age of ten, she delivered a speech at a TEDx event in Bhilwara, India, called 'Why You Don't Have to Wait Till You Grow Up'. She is also the organizer of a TEDx event at her school, making her the youngest TEDx Youth event organizer in Asia, and a noted public speaker who has delivered talks at TED Youth in New York City, TEDx events and education conferences like the Mind Mingle Festival for educators in Ahmedabad, India where she delivered this speech.

Ishita issued a call to live in the present for the sake of helping students achieve their full potential; instead of always focusing on the future, she pointed out that educators could instead see the possibilities of students taking action in the present.

Living in the Present to Create a Better Future

Mind Mingle Festival, Ahmedabad, India · 2016

In doing [many things for happy lives and careers] sometimes we forget about the present. We forget about right now... That reminds me of an interview ... with the Dalai Lama. The interviewer asks the Dalai Lama, 'Who or what do you think is the most strange, unusual or weird thing in this universe?' He responds by saying, 'It's man.' The interviewer is in awe: 'Why? How?' The Dalai Lama explains it is man because he sacrifices his health in order to make money, then he sacrifices money to recuperate his health, and then he is so anxious and nervous about the future he does not enjoy the present. The result: he does not live in the present or the future. He lives as if he is never going to die, and he dies having never really lived.

I am only a child and I don't have all of the solutions. But I want you all to realise, neither do you. This is not to offend anyone, but for all of you to realise that the future we are building – by doing what we are in the present – does not look too good to me ... The next time you talk to a young person like me, instead of asking them what they want to be when they grow up, please ask them what they want to be now. I think educators play a very big role in a student or child's life. The purpose of education is to make minds, not careers. I think if educators can ask the question, 'What do you want to be now?' to everyone, the world could be changed. The question 'What do you want to be when you grow up?' has an inherent problem: it diminishes what a young person can do today. It encourages the child to wait until a future time to do what he or she wants to do today. Why? ... We need to be true to ourselves.

Hadiqa Bashir

ACTIVIST AGAINST CHILD MARRIAGE

Hadiqa Bashir, an activist from Pakistan, has been raising awareness in her community – and around the world – about the negative effects of child marriage. Hadiqa herself suffered pressure from her grandmother to marry at the age of eleven, only narrowly avoiding this thanks to support from a sympathetic uncle, the rights activist Erfaan Hussein Babak. Her grandmother was furious and the disagreement led to a months-long estrangement between them but it did not dissuade Hadiqa from her next move: campaigning to ensure that no girl would have to go through such a situation ever again.

Hadiqa decided to begin going door-to-door in her neighbourhood to speak to families about stopping to think before marrying off their daughters. At the age of fourteen, with her uncle's help, she founded an organization called Girls United for Human Rights. It works to save hundreds of girls from losing their futures to early marriage by instead helping them into education. This is challenging work, since Hadiqa has to fight deeply embedded patriarchal societal norms that make child marriage seem acceptable, and even desirable. Some members of her community have interpreted the Koran in such a way as to argue that child marriage is also condoned by the Muslim faith. Hadiqa disagrees, pointing to passages that prohibit forcing women into marriages against their will. Challenging patriarchy and others' religious interpretations is deeply fraught, and not without controversy, but while it may be an uphill battle to change her neighbours' minds, Hadiqa has received accolades and encouragement from supporters around the world. In 2015, she became the youngest ever winner of the Muhammad Ali Humanitarian Award in 2015.

Hadiqa said in her 2016 speech, 'I believe that the biggest award will be that a real change takes place and that every girl of my age is in school, instead of being forced into marriage. The effect you have on others is the most valuable currency there is. Believe in yourself. One human being, with conviction, can bring real change.'

Early and Forced Marriage

National Youth Event, Lake Buena Vista, Florida, USA • 2016

In my community, we have a tradition of little girls playing with their dolls ... and marrying their dolls with a small celebration. I was seven years old when one of my friends told me that she [was] getting married. All our friends were very excited when we thought of the celebration and dressing up. At the time, we were too young to understand what was happening. For us, it was a doll wedding come to life ...

One day, we arranged a party for her at school. She did come but was very pale and down. We saw wounds on her arms and asked her what happened. She started crying and told us that her husband beat her with an iron wire. We were in shock ... She was just eight years old ...

My friend's face haunted me for months. Then, when I turned eleven, a marriage proposal came for me ... My grandmother told my father to say yes ... My father also seemed satisfied. I started crying. I could not believe that my father, who always supported me for getting education, was now ready to get me married off at this age. I ran to my uncle and told him everything ... He told me about child marriage laws. I bravely told my father and grandmother that I would fight a child marriage case against them in the court of law ... My uncle supported me and told my family that child marriage is a crime. It was only then that my family realised that what they were doing is wrong. That one bold step changed my whole life.

... I was thinking about my education. I never wanted to live like a slave and get beaten like an animal. All these events forced me to think that someday when I will be on my deathbed, standing around my bed will be the ghost of the ideas, the dreams, abilities, given to me by life. If I for whatever reason never acted on those ideas – never pursued those dreams, never used my leadership skills, never used my voice – then they would stand around my bed ... with large angry eyes [saying], 'We came to you, and only you could have given us life, but now we must die with you forever?' I was never ready to be haunted by these questions.

... I asked myself, what role could I play, what could be done, and how should I act to bring about change in my society for young girls? I believed in myself, and I decided that I will fight and that I would spread awareness regarding this cruel act. I adopted a multi-pronged strategy for raising community awareness on issues of early and forced marriages by visiting door to door, and telling mothers, fathers, uncles, aunts and grandparents about the impact of early and forced marriages on girls' reproductive and mental health, economic deprivation and lack of education. Now, I meet with the legislators and persuade them to speak on the assembly floor about girl-friendly legislation.

That one bold step changed my whole life.

———

Hadiqa Bashir

Age 14

Schuyler Bailar

TRANSGENDER RIGHTS ADVOCATE AND SWIMMER

Schuyler Bailar is a competitive swimmer at Harvard University. Assigned female at birth, Schuyler grew up as a 'water baby', learning how to swim at the same time as learning how to walk, and swimming competitively from the age of four.

After suffering bullying in elementary and middle school for not conforming to gender expectations, Schuyler tried to fit into high school, while also getting good grades and making national records in swimming that earned attention from Harvard's women's team coach and a place on the team.

Despite being successful on the surface, Schuyler struggled with mental illness and self-harm, leading him to take a gap year and seek therapy. It was at that time that he came out as transgender, including to the coach of Harvard's women's team. In his speech at an event hosted by *The Economist*, Schuyler told the story of deciding whether or not to swim for the men's team after his transition. He shares his own personal journey to show young people they do not need to sacrifice their identities in order to succeed at the sports they love.

My Journey *The Economist's Voices*
from the Frontlines event, London, UK • 2017

When I was sitting in the office of the [Harvard] women's team coach and she told me I had the option to swim for either [the men's or women's] team ... I burst into tears. They were not tears of relief or happiness or even excitement. I was terrified ... Because now I've got to pick between these two options. With everything I feel like I've ever worked for on this female side—hopes of breaking Harvard records, going to nationals, maybe going for Olympic trials—this was everything I'd worked for my whole life. And on the other side I have the potential to be happy, starting all over again as a male athlete, and working for something ... completely new ... The women's coach said, 'Schuyler, you're at the edge of a cliff. You've actually got a safety harness on, even though you don't know it. And you just have to jump. You have to take that risk.' I wrote her an email and said, 'I think I'm going to jump.' And so I did.

Swimming at my first meet as male, I remember standing before the race for the national anthem ... With my hand over my heart, I realized there was no strap between my hand. I always used to put one finger on either side of the strap of my women's suit, and now I only had a Speedo on. I realized in that moment everything was different, because for the first time in my life I was swimming as myself. Wholly unrestrained, just me. Which was a pretty incredible feeling.

That's why I'm so passionate about sharing my story ... because when I was little, I didn't have LGBTQ role models or athletes to look up to and think, 'I can be me' ... So I share my story (not me as in Schuyler but me as a trans athlete) because I want people to know that they can do what they love and be who they are.

Troye Sivan

SINGER-SONGWRITER, ACTOR, AND
LGBTQ+ RIGHTS ACTIVIST

Troye Sivan, a South African-born Australian pop singer-songwriter and actor, is internationally recognized for a slew of hit songs; his single 'Youth' made it to #23 on the Billboard Hot 100 – the United States' music industry standard record chart – and his 2018 album *Bloom* reached #4 on the Billboard 200. In addition to his prolific discography, Troye has acted in films like *X-Men Origins: Wolverine* and *Boy Erased*.

Troye came out to millions of fans with a vlog he posted on his YouTube channel in 2013 at the age of eighteen; since then, he has spoken out often about the importance of queer visibility. In an interview in the *Kitchener Post*, he said, 'Being a gay guy myself, I have such vivid memories of the few times I saw any type of LGBTQ relationship on TV or in music videos. I did see an opportunity to try and make change.' Troye has spoken publicly about striving against internalized homophobia, spreading awareness about the issue of homelessness among LGBTQ youth (40 per cent of homeless youth in the US identify as LGBTQ), addressing myths about HIV/AIDS, and promoting LGBTQ representation in his music videos.

Although Troye has received numerous accolades for his activism, he is quick to use his platform to point out the complex nature of power and privilege, and the lesser-known figures who might deserve more attention. In an interview with the publication *Another Man*, he said, 'I come from a middle-class white family in Australia, and all of my dreams have come true by twenty-two. I had the easiest coming out in the world ... there are plenty of other people who need to be heard first.' When the American non-profit organization GLAAD, which advocates for LGBTQ people in the media, awarded him with their Stephen F. Kolzak Award, Troye used the opportunity to amplify the names and work of numerous activists who had come before him.

Please don't let anyone strip you of your truth and your love, because those are the foundations of who we are as a community.

———

Troye Sivan

Age 21

GLAAD's Stephen F. Kolzak Award Acceptance Speech

GLAAD Media Awards, Los Angeles, USA • 2017

About a year or two ago, I watched a documentary called *How to Survive a Plague*. The doc is about the early years of the AIDS epidemic and the efforts of organisations like ACT UP and the Treatment Action Group. Within the characters in the doc, I saw myself and I saw my friends and I saw my colleagues and I saw my boyfriend ... The difference was that these people were attending a friend's funeral on a weekly basis. This was in New York City not even forty years ago. They were fighting for medical treatment, for visibility and their lives—it was a life or death situation. In the documentary, you see the kids taking the ashes of their loved ones who had fallen victim to the AIDS epidemic and throwing them across the White House lawn just to be recognised ... This documentary shook me to my core; it was this kind of activism and sacrifice that paved the way for all of us to be here tonight.

... And so while I'm so thankful and fortunate to have this award, I would like to share it with the warriors who made it possible but maybe didn't get one for themselves. So this award is for Peter Staley, one of the featured activists in *How to Survive a Plague*. Peter was one of the driving forces behind ACT UP, the founder of the Treatment Action Group, and a personal hero of mine. This is for Marsha P. Johnson and Sylvia Rivera, the godmothers of the Stonewall riots who also founded a transgender rights group in the 1970s. This is for Bayard Rustin. Bayard was

an openly gay civil rights leader who worked alongside Martin Luther King Jr and was largely written out of history because of homophobia. This is for Gilbert Baker, the creator of the rainbow flag, a symbol of pride, who we sadly lost yesterday. This is for the Edie Windsors and the James Baldwins and the Frank Kamenys of the world, and the list goes on.

... Though times and our needs may have changed, this ethos and spirit still persists in our community today ... This is for every volunteer at an HIV clinic around the world, this is for staff at LGBTQ+ homeless shelters around the world working to get our youth into safe spaces ... for every parent who truly loves and supports their kid whoever they are. That's where the real glory lies ...

I'm lucky enough to play shows and see the young faces of our community when I do, and let me tell you, our future is so, so bright. Please don't let anyone strip you of your truth and your love, because those are the foundations of who we are as a community. In a time where it might be tempting to retreat into the shadows, I ask you to please be louder, keep holding hands, keep finding pride in your identity, keep standing up for those in our community who are most vulnerable, keep love in your heart and don't forget to share it with the world, because that love is something to be so proud of, and something that no one can ever take from us.

Gavin Grimm

TRANSGENDER YOUTH RIGHTS ADVOCATE

When Gavin Grimm came out as transgender at the beginning of high school, his parents reacted with love and support, and his school initially respected his gender identity. However, everything changed when the local school board held a meeting to discuss whether or not Gavin should be allowed to use the boys' restroom at school, without informing the Grimm family. Some in the community argued that those assigned female at birth should be forced to use the girls' restroom, even if that did not align with their gender identity, and the school board capitulated. Gavin sued the school board for discrimination. His case went all the way to a federal judge in Virginia. The school board tried to get the case dismissed, but the judge ruled in Gavin's favour, writing that his school district's bathroom policy had discriminated against him. However, that victory came in 2018, after Gavin had already graduated from high school.

One of the most contentious issues surrounding trans students and their rights at school is bathroom usage – specifically, whether students should be allowed to use bathrooms corresponding to their gender identity. For Gavin, a transgender student, this debate was more than fodder for political discussion; it was deeply personal, as it affected his health and wellbeing while attending classes at Gloucester High School in Virginia. The Obama administration had issued guidance to primary and secondary schools receiving federal funding around the nation intended to protect the rights of trans students, but the Trump administration chose to roll back those protections in 2017.

That was a catalyst for elected officials in the House of Representatives organizing a forum on civil rights under the Trump administration. They invited Gavin to speak out about his own experiences, the ramifications of being made the subject of public discussions in front of his school board, and the importance of continuing to protect trans children.

Statement of Gavin Grimm, Plaintiff in G.G. v. Gloucester County School Board, for 'Civil Rights Under the Trump Administration – The First 100 Days' Forum

Washington, D.C., USA • 2017

At the end of my freshman year, I got the courage to tell my parents something that I had known for a long time. I told them that I am transgender and that I am a boy. They had nothing but love and support for me.

By the time school started, I had transitioned and was finally living as my true self ... My principal told me that I was free to use the boys' restrooms ... This was, unfortunately, a false sense of security. After this seven-week period, the school board held a meeting—a public conversation about my genitals and restroom usage—without even notifying me or my family. My mother and I found out by chance less than twenty-four hours before the meeting was to happen ...

I went to that meeting and spoke about why it was important to me—as a boy—to live life like other boys do, including being able to use the boys' bathroom at my school. Family and a few close friends stood by me, but nothing could have prepared me for what was to come. People speaking out against me made a point of referring to me with female honorifics and pronouns. They warned me that I was going to be raped or otherwise abused ... At a second meeting, a month later, the rhetoric was even more inflammatory. Word had spread throughout the community and people turned up in droves. After each frenzied remark, clapping and hollering reverberated throughout the room ... I sat while my school board voted to banish me to retrofitted broom closets or the nurse's room ...

My school board had invalidated me in perhaps the most humiliating way possible. But two years later ... I stand stronger and prouder than ever ... My case will not be resolved until after I graduate. But this fight is bigger than me. This fight is for other trans youth in my high school ... It [is] for all trans youth who are in school or one day will be. It is for the friends and loved ones of these youth, who want these children to be happy and healthy, rather than at risk and in danger as so many trans people are.

It is for these reasons that I was so disappointed earlier this year when the Trump administration withdrew critically important guidance to schools throughout the nation regarding the civil rights of trans students ... On the night the Trump administration withdrew this guidance, I stood with hundreds outside the White House to speak out against this action. While we stood there, in both anger and heartbreak, I was nonetheless inspired by the tremendous outpouring of support for trans students. Signs saying 'Protect Trans Kids' and 'I Stand With Trans Students' were everywhere.

Actions do speak louder than words, and the message that night was clear: regardless of what obstacles come before me and other trans students, regardless of what hatred or ignorance or discrimination we face, we will be fine because we have love on our side.

...regardless of what hatred or ignorance or discrimination we face, we will be fine because we have love on our side.

Gavin Grimm

Age 17

Tiera Fletcher (née Guinn)

ROCKET DESIGN AND ANALYSIS ENGINEER

Tiera Fletcher is working on the engine for NASA's space launch system programme that will send humans to Mars. At the age of twenty-two she told her youth audience in a packed stadium at WE Day, a day-long event intended to motivate youth to participate in volunteer efforts: 'It's the largest rocket ever created in history.' The rocket is expected to weigh 188,000 pounds (or about 85,275 kilos) and stand 322 feet (over 98 meters) tall.

When Tiera was as young as six, she already loved numbers and building things, turning to materials like LEGO, construction blocks, construction paper, pencils, coloured pencils and crayons to translate her dreams into drawings on the page or physical objects. A few years later, her passion for aerospace engineering started. At the age of eleven, she participated in a programme at her elementary school that gave her the chance to explore different aspects of engineering; subsequently, she 'fell in love' with aerospace. After graduating from the Massachusetts Institute of Technology (MIT) and beginning work full-time at

Boeing, Tiera met and married a fellow aerospace engineer named Myron Fletcher. Together they post content under the title 'Rocket with the Fletchers' about research, science and engineering, increasing the representation of minority engineers online and acting as role models for the next generation of innovators.

As one of a small group of African-American women in aerospace engineering, Tiera is passionate about shining a light for others; she encouraged her audience at WE Day to consider ways they could help change the status quo and help increase women's representation in various professions. Tiera has received numerous accolades for her work, including MIT's Albert G. Hill Prize for high academic performance and work to improve life for minorities on campus and 'Most Promising Engineer' from the 2019 Black Engineer of the Year awards.

Getting to Boeing and NASA was not easy. No dream ever is. You always have to fight to achieve them. It requires focus and determination.

Tiera Fletcher

Age 22

Twenty-two-year-old NASA Rocket Engineer

WE Day, Seattle, Washington, USA · 2017

As you can see, I'm a young woman of color. In the aerospace field that, despite incredible progress, makes me a triple minority. There is a dangerous and looming trend in the conversation around feminism: the belief that we have 'achieved' equality, the notion that we no longer need feminism. That has to stop. The women before us were courageous and impactful but it is dangerous for us to think that we have arrived. It is in the moments of rest that progress stops and we move backwards. Although women's representation and status in various professions is growing, the gender gap persists and the number of us in science continues to lag behind men. But we have the power to change that, right?

... At six years old, I wanted to be a mathematician. Every trip to the grocery store, my mom would give me the clipped coupons and then by the time we reached the register I'd have to calculate the exact total, including tax. Then, I wanted to be an inventor, a scientist, an architect, and not long after, I wanted to design planes and rockets. I nurtured my love of math and science at various summer programs and afterschool activities,

inching me closer and closer to my goals ... I worked hard and studied even harder and now I'm pursuing a degree in aerospace engineering at MIT.

... Getting to Boeing and NASA was not easy. No dream ever is. You always have to fight to achieve them. It requires focus and determination. But women are powerful and no one can say otherwise ... The fight for equality isn't solely in the numbers, it's in the small success stories—like a young girl excited about math in the supermarket, or an engineer in the making always looking forward to building a rocket to send humans to Mars ... We all have the power to change the world, whether that's preparing humanity for the epic trip to Mars or simply raising awareness about a cause that is close to your heart. So empower the girls and young women in your lives to achieve their dreams, encourage curiosity, permeate a sense of wonder and support the aspirations of others. And most importantly, believe in yourself.

TIERA FLETCHER (NÉE GUINN) 93

Melati and Isabel Wijsen

ENVIRONMENTAL ACTIVISTS

Melati and Isabel Wijsen are sisters from Indonesia who have made it their mission to eliminate plastic bags from their home island of Bali, protecting the oceans that humanity relies upon. They delivered this speech at the United Nations' World Ocean Day when Melati was sixteen and Isabel was fourteen.

Plastic, which we use every day in forms ranging from the straws in cold drinks to the takeaway containers holding salads, is convenient, cheap and disposable. However, it is also slowly poisoning Planet Earth. In August 2019, scientists in Colorado's Rocky Mountains found plastic fibres in rain falling from the sky. And according to the Ocean Conservancy, eight million metric tons of plastics enter the ocean annually. That is in addition to the estimated 150 million metric tons that already circulate right now in our marine environments.

Founding Bye Bye Plastic Bags at the ages of twelve and ten after being inspired by a lesson on key historical figures at school, Melati and Isabel aim to make clear the consequences of human behaviour. They have taken their message to venues around the world, sharing their personal love of the ocean nurtured by growing up on an island, while also delivering calls to action that remind audiences the time for action is now.

Melati and Isabel's activism helped to raise awareness and increase pressure on the government in Bali to do something about the epidemic of trash surrounding their island. On 24 December 2018, Bali governor I Wayan Koster announced a ban of single-use plastic – everything from straws to shopping bags. The plastic industry challenged the ban in court but found its suit rejected by Indonesia's Supreme Court, an important victory for the nation's environmental activists hoping to enact similar bans in more locales.

Powerful people have been paying attention to the Wijsen sisters' activism beyond their home shores, too: media organizations such as Forbes, *TIME* magazine, and CNN have listed them among the world's most influential teenagers, and Isabel and Melati have spoken at TED, the International Monetary Fund World Bank Forum and the United Nations.

... we stand here today because we do not have the luxury to wait until someone else takes action or until we become the leaders.

Melati Wijsen

Age 16

Speech at World Oceans Day 2017

World Oceans Day 2017, United Nations Headquarters,
New York City, USA · 2017

MW: For as long as I can remember, the ocean has been a part of our lives ... is a part of all of our lives. Not only does it produce 70 per cent of the oxygen we breathe, but the ocean is also responsible for more than three-and-a-half billion people who still depend on it as a primary source of food. And it supports more than 80 per cent of life on Earth. So you can begin to ask yourself the question: why [do] we still treat our oceans so badly?

IW: Maybe because it's easy to do ... Maybe we didn't know the alternatives. But today we do ...

MW: Saying no to plastic bags is the first step. Then waste management. Then a clean sea. Simple, and maybe naive of us kids to think that way, but definitely not as complicated as everyone seems to pretend it is. It is not rocket science, but a change in mindset. It is shifting your mindset one bag at a time.

IW: We started Bye Bye Plastic Bags [with] no plan, no hidden agenda, no greed. Actually, I think we had no idea what we were up against. We had [the] pure intention to get people on the island of Bali to say no to plastic bags. We have been campaigning for almost five years now ... working from the bottom to the top and the top to the bottom. We have spoken to ... students, in twelve different countries, and in eight different languages ...

MW: And so we stand here today to show ... that youth can be more than an inspiration ... Allow us to drive the decisions that you are making today. Allow us youth to be the voice that motivates your approaches for the solutions that create the world we want to be a part of. And we stand here today because we do not have the luxury to wait until someone else takes action or until we become the leaders. We are here now and we are ready. The time for change has never been better.

Xiuhtezcatl Martinez

ENVIRONMENTAL ACTIVIST AND MUSICIAN

Xiuhtezcatl Martinez is an indigenous American climate activist who advocates for environmental protection as Youth Director of Earth Guardians. He has spoken at venues including United Nations climate summits, and began his public speaking at the age of six, when he delivered a two-minute speech at a national event about global warming incorporating a traditional Native American prayer. His speeches have brought attention to the intersections of ecological destruction and other structural forms of oppression, such as those affecting indigenous communities in the United States.

In his home state of Colorado, he joined with other young people affiliated with the organization Our Children's Trust, to sue state and federal government agencies over their failure to act decisively on global warming; Martinez served as the lead plaintiff in a legal challenge to the Colorado Oil and Gas Conservation Commission over issuing approvals to energy companies engaged in fracking (hydraulic fracturing, the process of extracting oil and gas through injecting liquid into the earth at high pressures). He has also spoken widely about the need for an intersectional approach to climate justice.

In addition to his repertoire of activism and public speaking, Xiuhtezcatl is a hip-hop artist who blends music and consciousness-raising about environmental justice. In his speech at the Aspen Ideas Festival, he advised young people that making change in the world is not only about conventional activism or community organizing; it can also begin with looking inward and identifying one's passion and joys – in his case, for the musical arts.

What do I love in this world, how can I engage [with] that to make a difference?

———————————

Xiuhtezcatl Martinez

Age 17

We Have the Power to Shape Our World

Aspen Ideas Festival, Colorado, USA · 2017

I'm seventeen years old, I'm a climate activist, I'm a spokesperson for my generation, I've been involved in the climate justice movement for a really long time ... There's often this misconception that the power to create change in the world will come from other people, hoping and waiting that they'll take action on our behalf, but I firmly believe that the greatest change we will ever see in the world will come from young people ... I'm so excited to ... continue to see more young people all over the planet stepping up ... and [exhibiting] acts of leadership.

Along with being a frontline climate activist and a spokesperson ... I'm also an artist. I'm an MC, a hip-hop artist, and I think it's incredibly crucial to realize that talking about an issue like climate change is not just talking about the environment. There are so many different issues that are connected, from racial justice to economic justice, understanding that climate change threatens poor women and children of color more than anyone else ... and seeing indigenous communities at the front lines of

our environmental crisis. This issue is incredibly diverse. If you look at environmental activism over the past several years it has not been as exciting as it could be, so I think diversifying the way in which we talk about these issues and the way we take action is incredibly important.

We are seeing artists standing up and using their platforms ... I saw Ms Lauryn Hill and Common, and Common was doing a really dope set ... about racial justice and how he hasn't found success in his career until he's found racial justice for his people, his communities. [He said this] in front of 10,000 people at Red Rocks [a venue in Colorado]. He's using music to inspire and create change. Rather than just thinking, 'How can we be a more successful activist or community organizer?' ... we can look within and say 'What am I good at? What am I passionate about? What do I love in this world, how can I engage [with] that to make a difference?' So I'm going to play some music for you guys.

Elijah Walters-Othman

ADVOCATE FOR EQUAL ACCESS TO EDUCATION AND JOB TRAINING

At the age of seventeen, Elijah Walters-Othman was deeply frustrated by UK politics. The country had just voted in the Brexit referendum to leave the European Union and he worried that youth – especially those from less privileged backgrounds – were not involved enough in the political process. Asked in an interview why young people were not participating in politics, Elijah expressed concern about 'the distance from those in power. They feel very alien: from the clothes, to the private education, to the privilege. Many working-class young people can't relate to them, so there's a massive distance – geographically, too, for us in Manchester. When you go to a private school, you're told from a young age that you'll be a leader of society. In state schools, we aren't given those high expectations. We're just left to our [own] devices.'

In 2017, he cofounded a youth campaign collective, an arm of the charity organization Reclaim, called 'Team Future', hoping to draw more youth into political organizing. That same year, while still seventeen, Elijah was elected to be a Member of the UK Youth Parliament (a youth organization that holds democratic elections for new members every year). He quickly took on his mandate to represent the youth of Manchester with a speech on the importance of equality of opportunity, no matter your postcode.

When Elijah gave his 2017 speech, the Youth Parliament was discussing the possibility of creating an online 'work experience hub' for young people between eleven and eighteen. The hub would act as a clearing house for opportunities that would give them real-world experiences, enhancing their education and making them more attractive applicants to employers later on. The idea behind such a hub would be to help eradicate some of the disparities that otherwise exist between youth in rich and poor, urban and rural areas. Beyond his call for equality, Elijah's speech speaks to the power of dreams and the importance of resisting discouraging messages from society.

The Difference Between Dreams and Reality Is Action

UK Youth Parliament Debate, British House of Commons,

London, UK • 2017

The difference between dreams and reality is action. It appears that the very essence of youth is built upon our passion to dream, our resolve to strive and an everlasting effort to overcome our trials in a society that often tells us, 'No, you can't.'

Work experience hubs, by convention, are there to bridge the gap between education and the world of work. But what if I told you that that is only the echo of a convention broken by misguided opportunity, failed dreams and the means to tell our young people to never look beyond the life they have been given? So when 65 per cent of employers believe work experience to be critical for employment and only 38 per cent are willing to offer it, surely something has to change?

In 2012 ... young people were told that because of the school we attend there was no obligation to offer work experience. With those words, inequality of opportunity only persists. We should no longer have to live in a society in which we are defined by where we live, what our parents earn and, especially, by an education system that has failed the many generations that came before us. In our actions today, we can break the cycle.

... My home is Manchester, and I remember growing up with my friends and dreaming that we could be doctors or lawyers – there was even one who believed they could be an astronaut ...

I was once told that a postcode should never have to dictate potential so, with those words, I stand before you today with a belief: I believe that a young person on the streets of Moss Side deserves the exact same opportunity as a young person at Eton; I believe that a young person from the tower blocks of Lewisham deserves the exact same opportunity as a young person from Westminster; and I believe that the young person who feels isolated in the rural areas of this country deserves the exact same opportunity as a young person from Harrow ...

Let us be remembered as the young people who voted for work experience hubs for the young people of this country.

... the very essence of youth is built upon our passion to dream, our resolve to strive and an everlasting effort to overcome our trials, in a society that often tells us, 'No, you can't.'

Elijah Walters-Othman

Age 17

Muzoon Rakan Almellehan

CHILDREN'S EDUCATION ADVOCATE
AND UNICEF GOODWILL AMBASSADOR

Fighting in Syria has taken a vast human toll, causing an estimated 511,000 deaths as of March 2018 (Syrian Observatory for Human Rights), with 6.6 million people internally displaced and another 5.6 million displaced around the world (UNHCR). However, before the headlines of death and destruction people around the world saw on their television screens, many men, women and children lived ordinary lives – simply going to work and school, looking forward to futures for themselves and their families.

For education advocate Muzoon Rakan Almellehan, the onset of civil war meant that she had to leave all the comforts of home behind for an uncertain future in a refugee camp when she was in ninth grade. 'The only belongings I took were my schoolbooks,' she recalled of that time.

Muzoon and her family lived in refugee camps for three years, including eighteen months in the Za'atari refugee camp in Jordan. While there, she began working with UNICEF to campaign for the rights of children to access education. Fellow education advocate Malala Yousafzai specifically looked for Muzoon when she visited Za'atari, having heard of her work to ensure more children – especially girls – stayed in education.

As Muzoon describes in her speech for the Glamour Awards, one of the saddest consequences of the violence in Syria was the loss of hope and potential for all the young people who saw their educations interrupted, sometimes with no hope of resuming, because of war. For many young women and their families, hopelessness about the future translated into education being an impossible dream and sometimes even entering into marriage at young ages. Determined to do something, Muzoon began speaking out around the refugee camp – and, later, in public venues around the world – with a plea for equal educational access for Syria's girls.

Muzoon and her family were moved to Newcastle, UK, in late 2015, where she and her siblings were enrolled in a local school.

When I raise my voice, I raise my voice for them.

Muzoon Rakan Almellehan

Age 18

Speech for Glamour Awards

Glamour Women of the Year, Brooklyn, USA · 2017

I am so humbled and so honoured to be here today with all the Glamour Women of the Year. All of you are incredible leaders and activists fighting for a world where we can live in peace and free from oppression.

We all have our own stories and our own reasons behind what inspires our fight for justice and equality, and I'd like to share mine with you.

In February 2011, the Syrian war began. The years that followed saw the destruction of my beautiful country, the death of my family members and friends, the displacement of so many children, and the war that has resulted in millions of Syrian children being forced out of school.

For a short time, I was one of those children.

It's an unthinkable amount of hope and potential stolen because of war. In February 2013, the violence became too much. I didn't want to leave, but to survive we had to. In one day, I left behind my school, my friends, my aunt, my uncle, my neighbours, and everything I knew. The only things I carried were my schoolbooks and a book of memories my friends had made for me. As you can imagine, if someone had told me in that moment that I'd be standing on stage in front of you, telling my story, I would have thought they were joking. In that moment I thought my story would have ended in the refugee camps – the camps I was to call home for the next three years.

I'd always known that education is the key to everything, so when I arrived in the camp I found a school. I felt my hope was restored. I thought the first day would be the happiest since arriving in the camp, but it wasn't. I saw that so many girls were being forced into marriage and would miss out on school. This is when the activist in me started to rise. I went from tent to tent in the camp, talking to young people and their parents about the importance of education, persuading them to have hope for the future.

Since those days, I have a bigger platform. I am a UNICEF Goodwill Ambassador, but I am also still just a young person knocking on different kinds of doors, with the one mission of creating a world where children can learn in peace. I will always carry Syria in my heart, but the book of memories that my friends gave me is the only belonging I have from my life there. I sometimes look at that book, but only when I feel very strong, because it is so sad not to know where any of those friends are – the people I shared my childhood and so many hopes and dreams with. I don't know if they are alive. And if they are alive, I don't know if they did ever make it to school.

When I raise my voice, I raise my voice for them. I raise my voice for them and all children caught up in conflict, whose chance to go to school has been taken from them. I raise my voice for them because in the darkness, learning gives you light.

Josh Lafazan

LEGISLATOR AND POLITICAL ACTIVIST

Josh Lafazan already had a track record of giving back to his community before he was old enough to vote. In 2011, when he was seventeen years old, he became the Founder and CEO of Safe Ride Syosset, a community outreach programme aimed at preventing drunk driving by local teenagers by offering rides. When he was eighteen, Josh won an election to his local school board, a victory that made him the youngest elected official in the state of New York. After briefly attending community college so that he could remain close to home and carry out his school board duties without interruption, he transferred to Cornell University for his final years of school and subsequently finished a Master's degree at the Harvard Graduate School of Education.

Lafazan's passion for politics stems from his close attention to issues that affect the well-being of his constituents. In particular, he has paid attention to substance abuse, serving on the Board of Directors of the Long Island Council on Alcoholism and Drug Dependence (LICADD) and the Nassau County Heroin Prevention Task Force.

At just twenty-three years of age he won an election in his native Nassau County that made him that county's youngest ever legislator. In his inauguration speech, he thanked supporters who made his win possible, including teenage interns only a few years younger than him, and outlined his priorities as a legislator, including providing more accessible resources to help treat substance abuse and implementing policies to combat corruption in government. Already, he has passed legislation to establish a 24-hour hotline for substance abuse intervention and established a committee aimed at reducing veteran homelessness. He intends to use his own experiences to empower other youth, teaching a class at Long Island University on running for office as a young person.

... bringing people together from all walks of life, from all professional backgrounds, from all political affiliations, to work together towards a common pursuit of good and honest government.

———

Josh Lafazan

Age 23

Election Acceptance Speech

Nassau County, New York, USA • 2018

This was, by all means, a victory that cannot be singularly claimed by me as the candidate. On the contrary, this was a win that was only made possible because of everyone in this room tonight.

Thinking back to the campaign, I wanted to articulate an event in the race that underscored just what a team effort this was. And I was reminded of what we in the campaign office called 'Hell Week', or publicly what we call 'Independence Signature Week'. Having never gone through the signature process, we had no idea of just how long it took to get these signatures, or that you needed a notary present for every individual signature. So, with five days to go until the signature due date, I asked the central organizers how many signatures we had. The answer was around seventeen. Then I asked how many signatures we needed. The answer was 111. It gets worse. Then I asked how many signatures we really needed to ensure we had a significant legal buffer. The final answer came to 140.

So, you have two options here: you either admit defeat, fail to get the signatures and forfeit that party line, or you fight until the deadline to meet your quota. I sent a panic email to all of you, detailing our predicament, and asking you, in ninety-degree heat, to give up your summer weekend, to beg strangers to sign a piece of paper for someone they've never met. You answered my call. Attorneys and paralegals and office managers and bankers showed up in a steady stream, and one by one, on foot in blistering heat, walked with me for 96 hours straight. And, when all was said and done, we didn't get 140 signatures; we submitted 212, which was the 2017 Nassau record for legislators.

That week was a microcosm of what this campaign was all about. This was my first-ever race for partisan office. We couldn't afford a high-profile staff of key political operatives and expensive consultants. No, we put together a team of the most incredible teenagers you'll ever meet, of moms and dads, PTA members and Little League coaches, volunteer firefighters and retired senior citizens. And that's what made this thing so special. It's this theme, of bringing people together from all walks of life, from all professional backgrounds, from all political affiliations, to work together towards a common pursuit of good and honest government. That was truly beautiful, and something that I can only hope to replicate during these next two years in office.

I vow to never sacrifice doing what is right for political expediency. I vow to remain accessible to all residents, not just those with influence. I vow to never let confidence turn into arrogance, and to always remain open to constructive criticism and outside suggestions. I vow to continue to organize robust internship programs, so [as] to give young people not just a voice but an actual seat at the table. I vow to never allow frustration to mutate into cynicism, and to always maintain my sense of unbridled optimism. And I vow to always put my constituents first.

Zach Latta

TECHNOLOGIST AND FOUNDER OF HACK CLUB

Zach Latta is a non-profit founder who knows first-hand the life-changing power of learning to write code for computer programs. As a child he saw few appealing career options in his town on the outskirts of Los Angeles, and it was not until he found that he could build websites – and maybe even build websites that people liked – that he felt he had a sense of purpose. After developing popular app-based games in high school, he dropped out to work full-time in San Francisco, becoming the first engineer at a messaging app called Yo.

At the age of seventeen, Zach received a Thiel Fellowship, a two-year grant established by polarizing tech titan and PayPal co-founder Peter Thiel. The fellowship requires its recipients to not attend college (at least for the duration of the fellowship) in favour of independent pursuits, such as founding companies. Zach chose to use his fellowship term to start Hack Club, a non-profit network of coding clubs giving high school students the opportunity to start their own after-school groups to learn how to code. For his work on Hack Club, he was listed in the Forbes 30 Under 30, an annual list of standout entrepreneurs and activists under the age of thirty.

At the age of twenty, Zach spoke to the audience at San Francisco's Accelerate Good Global conference, an event for professionals interested in non-profit and social good work. He told his story and said that in the midst of worrisome statistics about the hopelessness of American youth, one outcome of Hack Club that makes him particularly proud is giving a sense of belief to its participants – the same sense of hope that he found through coding years ago.

Hack to the Future

Accelerate Good Global conference, San Francisco, California, USA · 2018

[Growing up], I was told I could have one of two jobs: I could either work at the oil refinery or at the military base. Now, I was raised by two idealistic social workers who above all taught me the Golden Rule: to treat other people how I wanted to be treated. As a kid who was trying to figure out who he is in the world, I couldn't see a future living with myself building weapons that killed people or helping ruin the environment. As a result, I felt lost. I thought I had no future.

... One night, I was on Google and I got remarkably lucky, because I discovered coding. I built ... lots and lots of terrible, terrible websites. After doing this for long enough, after having no friends that were interested in coding, never meeting anyone else that had written code before, I almost gave up.

... Everything changed when I had the opportunity to help make something people actually did want: this game called Graal. People loved Graal. People love Graal so much that they do ridiculous things, like make ridiculous music videos in the game about the game ...

This was this incredibly formative experience ... In the process of learning to code, I learned to be. I realized that I mattered. For the first time in my entire life, I saw a future for myself ...

When I finally made it to high school, I really struggled. I missed a lot of school; I was technically truant. And I dropped out after my freshman year. Instead of working at the gas station, because I knew how to code, I was able to work in the technology industry. When I was given $100,000 by an infamous technology billionaire to not go to college, instead of starting a for-profit like every other person in my class, I started a non-profit, because quite frankly coding changes lives and something as empowering as this shouldn't be left to chance. And that's exactly what we're doing today. In 2018—in 2018—still, 60 per cent of schools in this country don't offer any computing classes.

... I got lucky, and there is a version of my life where I didn't. That's why I started Hack Club. Hack Club helps high school students start the computer science programs they wish their schools offered ... [through] student-led clubs that meet weekly, typically after school for two hours. In these meetings, students learn how to code together. Everyone starts with no experience, and by the end of the first meeting everyone's launched their first website. By the end of the third, everyone's built their first game. By the end of the school year, everyone's launched dozens of projects, they've been to events hosted by other hack clubs in their community, and hopefully they feel part of a community. Our students go on to do amazing things ...

In 2017, we were able to take a bet on 10,000 students around the world. Two years ago, when we launched, Hack Club was a little idea ... Since, it's grown [in]to a movement.

I realized I mattered. For the first time in my entire life, I saw a future for myself.

Zach Latta

Age 20

Memory Banda

ACTIVIST AGAINST CHILD MARRIAGE

Child marriage – the formal or informal arrangement of marriage of a boy or girl under the age of eighteen – is a global problem. In South Asia, almost half (45 per cent) of all women aged twenty to twenty-four reported being married before the age of eighteen. Six of the world's ten countries with the highest rates of child marriage are in West and Central Africa, but child marriage also exists in high-income nations; consider that in 2014, 58,000 children were married in the United States, where laws in some states allow children to marry at any age with the permission of their parents or legal guardians.

For Memory Banda, a Malawian children's rights activist, the road to fighting the practice of child marriage began in a painfully personal place. She saw her community pushing dangerous rites of passage on to young women when her own sister was sent to an 'initiation camp'. These camps functioned as coming-of-age experiences for young girls as they entered puberty, meant to instil traditional values and gender norms. This took on frighteningly violent forms: at the camps, an older man would rape the girls in the name of 'sexual cleansing', teaching them how to have sex. This experience could have significant negative consequences after the incident itself, including trauma, pregnancy, physical injury and disease.

After being sent to one of these camps, Memory's sister became pregnant and married

young, prematurely ending the possibilities of attaining further education or a professional career. For Memory, this was an unacceptable price to pay. When her community exhorted her to attend an initiation camp herself, she refused.

After talking to many more young women whose lives had been adversely affected by child marriage, Memory, still a teenager, started campaigning in her home country of Malawi to end the practice. Through her work with NGOs such as the Girl Empowerment Network and Let Girls Lead, she has been collecting first-person accounts from young women speaking up against child marriage that she shares while lobbying lawmakers. Her campaign has also taken her to international stages like TED and the Oslo Freedom Forum.

Thanks to activists like Memory, in April 2017 Malawi's government passed a law banning child marriage and raising the minimum age to legally marry to eighteen. She says of her sister's daughter, 'The little girl knows what the mom went through. And I am pretty sure she also has greater hopes for her own future.' Ultimately, Memory's activism is not only about ending the cruel practice of child marriage; it is about freeing girls to dream.

I could be that girl that can rise up, defend the rights of my fellow young girls in my community.

Memory Banda

Age 20

Outlawing Child Marriage in Malawi

Oslo Freedom Forum, New York, USA • 2017

My little sister was only eleven years old when she was given away to get married.

... This made me angry, and I wanted to rise up, but it was hard ... There's so many traditions in African countries especially when young children they are reaching puberty stage, because they have to go through a series of rite of passage ... For my country, girls as young as ten, eleven, twelve, they have to go to the initiation camp ... there is a special day where a man from the community comes to the camp and sleeps with each and every girl at the camp in a tradition called sexual cleansing.

Imagine the trauma that these young girls have to go through for the rest of their lives. This is a reality that happens every day in African countries, especially my country. I had a lot of questions as I was growing up. I asked myself, 'Why can't a girl have her own choices?'

... I decided at the age of thirteen that I could be that girl to stand up. I could be that girl that can rise up, defend the rights of my fellow young girls in my community. I formed a network of my fellow young girls, and we approached the traditional leaders in my community. We approached them and we asked them to ban this kind of sexual ritual at the camp.

... We came up with a campaign to ask the government to raise the legal marriage age from fifteen to eighteen. It was a hard campaign because now it wasn't a community thing, it was a national level thing, and it means we have to deal with politicians ... I remember at some point we were like, 'Maybe we just have to give up.' But we never gave up because with collective voice bigger things turn out better. We went on with our campaign and it took years and years of campaigning. In 2015 the legal marriage age was raised from 15 to 18.

... I'm not going to sit down because there is more work that needs to be done ... We have to raise awareness at the community level to make sure that we let the community know that it is now illegal to marry off their daughters, their children.

And this is not all. We need to make sure that girls' education is supported all over the world and we have to make sure that girls' voices [are] heard over the issues that concern them ... Girls everywhere in the world need your support. Change is possible. But change is possible when you rise up and you fight for what you believe in. And change [comes] quicker when you work collectively.

Kadallah Burrowes

ARTIST AND ACCESSIBLE DESIGN ADVOCATE

Kadallah Burrowes is a new media artist who sees design as a pathway to a more accessible world. He was described by one writer as 'part artist, part coder, part director'. New media art is a broad category that includes artwork created with various kinds of technologies, encapsulating virtual reality (VR) experiences, video games, 3D printing and much more.

New media artists have existed as long as human beings have been producing innovative technology but the category is gaining more recognition with the emergence of high-profile practitioners and academic programmes. Kadallah took advantage of the existence of an interdisciplinary department in college to study new media arts during his academic career and drew ample inspiration not only from the unusual mediums available to him but also from his surroundings in urban China, where he studied for several years at NYU Shanghai before graduating in 2018. There, he majored in Interactive Media Arts, learning about everything from media theory to designing for people with disabilities.

He also took on several innovative arts projects, including an interactive documentary about fear and a music visualization piece. Kadallah tries to democratize access to new media art with his work. One of his most ambitious projects, entitled 'SUCKERS', is a location-based virtual reality docu-fiction series about vampires living in Shanghai that used QR [Quick Response] codes hidden around the city to unlock videos. Kadallah described that project on his website as 'something that would immerse audiences without needing a whole lot of expensive tech'. This commitment to accessibility contrasts with many new media artists, who might require cost-prohibitive technology setups for audiences to be able to view their work.

Kadallah's desire to make 'SUCKERS' and his other art projects accessible is part of a larger commitment to art that exists for the benefit of the many, rather than the few. In his speech for the Zaojiu Youth Conference organized by NYU Shanghai, Kadallah spoke about applying the principles of accessible design not only to solve societal problems and design user experiences, but also when creating art that transcends the boundaries of art museums and galleries.

Accessible Design – A Gateway to the Future

Zaojiu Youth Conference, NYU Shanghai, China · 2018

What exactly is accessible design? Accessible designers strive to create products and designs that aren't just usable by people with disabilities but specifically keep them in mind throughout the entire design process. However, one of the common mistakes that we as designers make while trying to create accessible designs is mistaking disability only for the things that physically handicap us ... rather than a broader definition that includes other ways in which society or other factors may place us at a disadvantage, such as mental illness or poverty.

A group that would fit into this expanded definition would be China's 10 to 60 million 'left-behind children'—kids whose parents must leave them in their hometowns while they themselves travel to larger cities in order to send funds back home. As a result of being separated from their parents for such extended periods of time, a huge side-effect is an increase in mental health problems, with nearly 50 per cent of all left-behind children reporting depression or anxiety and roughly 37 per cent disclosing that they have at some point considered suicide.

I first found out about this huge problem during my sophomore year when I traveled to Shenzhen in order to participate in an 'Internet of Good Things' hack-a-thon in which every team designed with left-behind children in mind. Our team came up with MANGO, a device ... gamifying the children's daily tasks and giving them the feeling that they were still interacting with their parents despite the miles between them. Every time they did a daily task that was assigned to them and

verified by a teacher or guardian, they would get a point, and similarly every time their parent did a task that was 'assigned' to them—such as going to work or doing laundry—they would get a point. In turn, the device ... gave kids a continual sense of connection to their parents as well as peace of mind to the parents without needing to constantly check in with the child's temporary guardian.

Beyond traditional user experience design, accessible design principles can still be applied to creating works of art. [In] universal design, work isn't necessarily created explicitly to empower individual groups but is designed to be equally accessible for all individuals.

Art museums often view artwork as a monetary commodity ... Luckily, because of the internet it has become much easier for artists to share their work ... By exhibiting work online, artists utilize universal design principles by making it possible for people to partake without spending money on a museum ticket or even needing to be in the same physical location. Before the internet, for decades street artists have attempted to democratize art by taking work out of museums and putting them where the public can see them.

Universal design principles can be thought of as an answer to questions currently being raised about the necessity for representation in media. By designing work that empowers all groups, rather than just those in the majority, more people will be able to identify with a work (making it more 'accessible').

In universal design, work isn't necessarily created explicitly to empower individual groups, but is designed to be equally accessible for all ...

Kadallah Burrowes

Age 22

Lauren Singer

ENVIRONMENTALIST AND INFLUENCER

Lauren Singer was an Environmental Studies major at New York University (NYU). In her senior capstone class, she saw a fellow classmate eating out of a plastic takeaway container and felt irritated by what she perceived as a callous disregard for the wastefulness of single-use plastic. She writes on her website, 'I would sit there and think, we are supposed to be the future of this planet and here we are with our trash, messing it up.' However, when she returned home, she noticed the ubiquity of plastic everywhere in her own house. She decided that she had to adjust her lifestyle to exemplify her values, and has since gained international recognition for the zero-waste lifestyle she has led since 2012. For Lauren, living zero-waste meant trying not to send any waste to landfills. The sum of the trash she has unavoidably generated during her over six-year commitment fits in a small, 16oz glass jar.

Lauren documents her journey with living zero-waste on a personal blog called Trash is for Tossers, as well as the Instagram account of the same name, where she has over 350,000 followers. She founded a company called Package Free that sells reusable materials like food containers, bamboo cutlery sets and steel straws to help others reduce their reliance on single-use plastics. The company's website reads, 'We believe that it should be easy to make choices that positively benefit the environment ... We can all take simple steps to reduce our waste.' In 2018, she spoke at a forum in Stockholm for people interested in building more sustainable food systems about the power of these individual choices to make a better planet.

How to Live a Zero-Waste Lifestyle

EATforum18, Stockholm, Sweden · 2018

Almost six years ago, I decided to stop making garbage and not send anything to landfill ... This happened because I was an Environmental Studies student at NYU. I deeply, passionately cared about the environment ... One day after class I went home to make dinner ... I opened my refrigerator and saw something I'd never seen before. Every single thing that was in my refrigerator was packaged in plastic. All of my lettuce, all of my drinks, all of my condiments. Everything ... I realized that every single thing I had in my bathroom was packaged in plastic. All of my cleaning products ... all of my clothes—because I was participating in fast fashion and so much of that is made from synthetic fibres or plastics.

... I had been an Environmental Studies major for four years ... but everything in my apartment was made of plastic ... Every single day, I was subsidizing the [oil and gas] industry I was opposing ... In thinking a little more, I realized: I have to stop using plastic ...

I had to make lots of changes in my life ... making all of my own beauty products, how to shop without any packaging at all, and a whole slew of other things to help me live a zero-waste lifestyle which I live now ... I wanted to align what I care about deeply, environmental sustainability, with my day-to-day actions ... There are so many things I can do as an individual to have a positive impact on the environment ...

Every single day, the average American makes about four and a half pounds of trash per person per day. That's about nine to ten kilos. Over the course of the six years of me living a zero-waste lifestyle, saying no to packaged food, having a shopping list and being prepared, buying in bulk, composting, my actions have led to me saving 8,212lb of trash from landfills ... or 18,067.5 kilos. What does that mean? ... Keeping anthropogenic methane from landfills ... Choosing the kinds of industries that I'm subsidizing, by going to farmers' markets and buying food from local farmers I can have conversations about the kind of labor they employ ...

My choices matter, and as individuals what we do matters and we are powerful ... What I want to show is that our collective actions make up the state of the world ... The moment we decide to take responsibility for the state of the world ... and personal responsibility for our actions and know the things that we do every single day have an impact ... is the exact moment that we can actually change the world.

My choices matter, and as individuals what we do matters and we are powerful. What I want to show is that our collective actions make up the state of the world.

Lauren Singer

Age 27

Sparsh Shah

DISABILITY RIGHTS ADVOCATE

Sparsh Shah, who also shares his music under the name Purhythm, is an American disability rights advocate, motivational speaker and musician. He derived the name 'Purhythm' from combining the words 'pure' and 'rhythm' because he describes his rap as family-friendly (pure) and also rhythmic. He has more than 300,000 followers on YouTube, and his cover of Eminem's song, 'Not Afraid', has received more than 14 million views, even drawing the attention of Eminem's record label, Shady Records, who tweeted about him after the video went viral on YouTube.

Sparsh has rapped and spoken in front of audiences young and old. Recently, he delivered a talk called 'Living a Message with Music' at Google's headquarters. There, he said, 'I've been blessed to have inspired so many people, to show them it doesn't matter what you go through, it matters where you want to get to.' Sparsh has also touched on the role of faith in his life, saying that his strong belief in God enables him to see the positives of his condition: 'I believe that when God closes one door, he always opens another. For me, when the door on my ability to walk and run was closed, then one to music was opened.'

Sparsh has been the subject of a short documentary film entitled *Brittle Bone Rapper*, so named because Sparsh lives with the brittle bone disease Osteogenesis Imperfecta (OI). OI is a condition that permanently affects individuals from birth. The disease affects the body's production of collagen, a necessity for bone strength, and at its most severe can lead to hundreds of fractures. The documentary covered Sparsh's experience receiving a spinal fusion operation, a surgery that helps correct spinal instability, in 2017. That same year, immediately after his surgery, Sparsh travelled to Los Angeles to receive the Champion of Hope award for his work on behalf of other people living with disabilities.

At the age of fifteen, he spoke at WE Day, sharing his personal journey of living life with this disease and maintaining his motivation through the adversity it presents (joking, 'You name it, I've broken it') to inspire his audiences to persevere and to not allow the terms other people use to define them.

Speech at WE Day

WE Day, New York City, USA • 2018

I'm fifteen years old and I have Osteogenesis Imperfecta, a rare and incurable genetic disorder that makes my bones fragile. I was born with almost forty fractures ... Fifteen years and 130 fractures later, I've realized that my purpose is bigger than my pain. And my ambition is stronger than my adversity. What am I trying to say? Disabilities are not definitions. Mine doesn't stop me from reaching my full potential. It's just given me a different perspective on life. That's what I always tell everyone—that I diss my disability.

... And hey, I know I can't do things the same way as everyone else. My parents have to lift me in and out of bed every day or when I go up the stairs at my friends' houses. But I just have to find what works for me, and find how I can shine my light, what helps me cope.

For me, that was none other than music. Not only has singing, song-writing and rapping helped me cope with my bad days, but it lets me share my feelings with everyone who might resonate with my story. In fact, when I started putting some of my covers up on YouTube, people from all over the world would send me messages that they were inspired by my music. In fact, someone once messaged me saying that she was at such a low point in her life and she felt so worthless that she was planning to take her own life but seeing my videos and hearing my story inspired her to turn her whole life around and keep fighting. Isn't that amazing?

So now, after finding that purpose, I now use my platform to inspire and encourage others to embrace who they are and to unleash their potential. I may have broken many bones but I know that the two things that will never break in my life are my voice and my spirit. I'm Sparsh, I'm fifteen years old, I'm a singer, song-writer, rapper and inspirational speaker from New Jersey. I have a great life, great friends and family, and an amazingly cute little brother who I love dearly. And I am not defined by my disability, I am defined by the terms that I give myself. So how do you define yourself?

Disabilities are not definitions. Mine doesn't stop me from reaching my full potential.

Sparsh Shah

Age 15

Amanda Southworth

MENTAL HEALTH ADVOCATE

Around the world, close to 800,000 people die by suicide every year – that's one life gone every 40 seconds. Mental health is an issue that affects everyone. However, social stigma can keep many people from speaking openly about mental health, fearing being called 'crazy', being perceived as dangerous and subsequently discriminated against or overlooked. One of the best ways to combat this dangerous stigma is through many people sharing their own stories.

Amanda Southworth is an advocate for greater mental health awareness and support. Her own lifelong struggles with mental illness led her to speak up on behalf of others struggling with depression, anxiety and thoughts of self-harm. By speaking publicly about her experiences and exhorting audience members to pay closer attention to mental health, Amanda contributes to a broader movement to de-stigmatize frank conversations about this issue. In her speech at the 2018 Pennsylvania Conference for Women, she engaged with the nuanced consequences of technology, pointing out that many websites use algorithms intended to optimize user engagement (sometimes, by presenting more and more extreme content in order to keep viewers on websites longer and collect more data on them). She provided the deeply personal example of watching a parent slide into right-wing extremism due to falsehoods peddled online. At the same time, technology provided her saving grace while in the throes of acute depression and anxiety; Amanda described finding purpose through building apps that give youth mental health resources (e.g. games and exercises that help with building resiliency in the face of challenges) and emphasized the importance of reaching out a helping hand instead of simply remaining a silent bystander in the face of hurt, bullying and oppression.

We have a responsibility, not only as women but as people on this earth, to make sure we destroy things that oppress us or those less fortunate than us.

———————————

Amanda Southworth

Age 16

Speech at the 2018 Pennsylvania Conference for Women

Philadelphia, Pennsylvania, USA · 2018

School had never really been a fun place for me. Growing up, I was bullied ... I developed anxiety and depression and an eating disorder halfway through my sixth grade year. By my seventh, I was writing suicide notes to my dad, and four years later I was diagnosed with one of the most severe forms of PTSD ... all before my seventeenth birthday.

... I found refuge ... in technology ... I realized I could create a place where people who were mentally ill could learn ... tools to sustain themselves until they could go to professionals of mental health. I built an app called AnxietyHelper which provides information, resources and cognitive-behavioral therapy to those who are struggling with mental illness, and I launched it when I was thirteen ... Each user I got was another reason to stay alive. To keep each of them safe, I got up at 6am, went to school, and worked on the app until one or two in the morning ... I started AnxietyHelper because I wanted people to be safe ...

When my [LGBTQ+] friends were the subjects of abuse, bullying, hate crimes and more ... I saw that people treated these crimes like they were the side effect of someone's sexuality ... After hearing my mom recommend to my lesbian friend a trip to conversion therapy while I was still in the closet, I decided to build a second app called Verena, which is a fully encrypted security system for members of the LGBTQ+ community. The app allows them to anonymously alert contacts in the event of an emergency, save incidents to report later, find safe places near them, have a timer to alert contacts with their location in case they don't make it home on time, and above it all it hides itself as a math help app in case an abusive parent or partner finds it.

... Last January, I left high school halfway through my sophomore year and decided to move to Los Angeles with my dad to escape my abusive mom ... I dedicated my life to using technology to help people, and I was given a $25,000 grant from Congress. I basically did what any normal teenager would do—I dropped out of high school and started my own non-profit software development company, Astra Labs, to continue helping people with technology. I created Astra because I wanted to make technology work for good ... We have over 83,000 users around the globe ...

Like the activists and advocates before me, I'm going to try and fix the systems that try and push me underneath them. But I can't do it alone. We have a responsibility, not only as women but as people on this earth to make sure we destroy things that oppress us or those less fortunate than us.

Amika George

ACTIVIST FIGHTING PERIOD POVERTY

Amika George does not think that menstruation is anything to be ashamed of. However, she does think that we should be ashamed about not doing more to ensure periods do not keep young people out of school. While a student in secondary school, Amika was horrified to discover period poverty – a term Global Citizen defines as 'the lack of access to sanitary products, menstrual hygiene education, toilets, hand-washing facilities, and, or, waste management' – and how it kept some students around the world, even in her home country of England, from being able to attend school one week out of every month.

She was likewise dismayed to see the apparent lack of action by any major political party on this issue, despite the fact that periods are experienced by half the population. Amika decided to take matters into her own hands, starting the #FreePeriods social movement in 2017 to raise awareness about period poverty

and advocate for free sanitary products in schools and universities, so that nobody misses out on an education because of a natural bodily process. The Free Periods website declares, 'The Scottish government has made history by ensuring free access to menstrual products in all schools, colleges and universities. The Welsh government has also pledged £1m to address period poverty. In England, we are being left behind.'

The #FreePeriods social movement gained traction both online and in the streets; actress Emma Watson even nominated Amika for *Teen Vogue*'s 21 Under 21. At the Wired Next Gen conference, a one-day event for youth in London, Amika spoke about the movement – everything from how she started campaigning to what it was like to protest outside the Prime Minister's house.

Even though we were protesting about something that is so awful, there was this amazing sense of solidarity and celebration.

Amika George

Age 19

Trailblazer Amika George on How She Built the #FreePeriods Social Movement

Wired Next Gen, London, UK • 2018

I was sitting at my breakfast table one day and I was reading an article on my phone ... I couldn't believe it when I read ... about girls having to miss school for one week every single month for the most ridiculous reason ... because they couldn't afford pads and tampons. Their periods were stopping them from going to school ...

I contacted my local MP ... and found nobody was really doing anything, which upset me. Being a teenager and living my life on social media, I decided to use the internet to start #FreePeriods, a petition on change.org ... The idea is that the girls on free school meals would get free menstrual products as well ... girls already identified as coming from low-income families, those most likely to be suffering from period poverty themselves ... In a couple of weeks [the petition] got over 2,000 signatures, and [at the time of the speech] has over 180,000 ...

When the general election was called ... in May [2017], I contacted political parties about period poverty ... and the Green Party, Lib Dems and Women's Equality parties implemented pledges to end period poverty in their general election manifestos ... We had the word 'period' in three manifestos, which I don't think has ever happened before ...

With a few friends I decided to organise the #FreePeriods protest outside Downing Street. [On the day of the protest] a sea of red came towards me ... there were 2,000 young people ... Everyone was holding these banners with period puns on them, and everyone was so excited, they wanted to be there and show the government just how angry we were about this massive issue ... Even though we were protesting about something that is so awful, there was this amazing sense of solidarity and celebration ... Because we literally screamed through Theresa May's bedroom, she did listen, and ... she gave £1.5 million to address period poverty in the UK, which is an amazing step forward but not a long-term and sustainable solution because that money is only for a year. I'm going to keep fighting until we have a provision in every secondary school for girls, so that everyone can get the education they deserve ...

The other thing the campaign is trying to address is the taboo and silence around periods ... Talk about periods if you have them or even if you don't, just start a conversation. It's really easy and it immediately makes people open up. Moving forward in this fight for gender equality, periods have to be a really big part of that ...

So the next time you see something online ... think 'it's actually up to me'. It could be periods or something else completely; there's always going to be someone who supports you, a friend, or someone on the other side of the world, who wants to see that change as much as you do ... and as the Free Periods protest proved, there's definitely strength in numbers. Talk to your friends about issues, set up an online petition, organise a protest, and tell people you want to see change.

Millie Bobby Brown

ACTRESS AND UNICEF GOODWILL AMBASSADOR

Millie Bobby Brown is a British actress, most critically acclaimed in her role as the character Eleven in the Netflix science-fiction television series *Stranger Things*. Hoping to use her considerable global platform for good, Millie became the youngest ever Goodwill Ambassador for the United Nations Children's Fund (UNICEF) in 2018, at the age of fourteen. Goodwill Ambassadors help advocate for UNICEF and children around the world to their fans, new audiences and powerful leaders around the world.

Millie has spoken out publicly about social issues important to her; at the 2018 Kids' Choice Awards, she devoted part of her acceptance speech to a message about gun violence, wearing a shirt bearing the names of the seventeen victims of the Parkland School shootings. She has also spoken out about bullying in schools, sharing her own story of being bullied while attending school in England and the longstanding issues with anxiety that experience caused.

Millie was included on a list of the most 100 influential people in the world by *TIME* magazine. She said in an interview with *Glamour*, 'Young people's lives are increasingly under pressure. First of all, I want to make sure that children are protected from violence and exploitation. I also want to combat the negativity on social media – I have experienced it – it's like a disease. It's negative hate that is genuinely so horrifying to me. Climate change is so important too. I was just in London and Greta [Thunberg] was speaking and she really inspires me.' In 2018, she delivered a speech accepting her role as a UNICEF Goodwill Ambassador, sharing her vision for helping children around the world and encouraging the audience to 'go blue' (UNICEF's colour) for World Children's Day.

Starting today, let's remind ourselves of our rights as children, and let's demand those rights – not just for ourselves, but for every child here.

Millie Bobby Brown

Age 14

Appointment as UNICEF Goodwill Ambassador

United Nations Headquarters, New York City, USA · 2018

Happy World Children's Day, everyone ...

It's a pleasure to be at the United Nations to celebrate World Children's Day, a day when we celebrate children using their voices on the issues that affect us all. That's why World Children's Day is so important for me. This is a day for us. It is also a huge, huge honour to be appointed UNICEF's youngest ever Goodwill Ambassador. Given UNICEF's global role as the world's leading voice for children and young people, to be the youngest ever Goodwill Ambassador for UNICEF is more than an honour; it's a powerful privilege. As the saying goes: with great power comes great responsibility.

... So today, I am officially stepping into my role ... and I'm committing to this promise: I will speak out for the millions of children and young people whose voices have been silenced for far too long. I will shine a light on the issues that vulnerable children and young people have suffered around the world, including representing them at places where they haven't yet had a seat at the table. And most of all, I will make sure children and young people know their rights, and I will do everything I can to empower them to be the change they want to see in the world.

... As I stand here now, millions of children do not have access to education. Millions don't have a safe place to call home. Millions don't have nourishing food, vaccines or clean water to keep them healthy or strong. It's my wish that every child, no matter where they live or the circumstances they were born into, have the chance to be heard. We have the passion, the fire and the ideas to make the change.

... In becoming a UNICEF Goodwill Ambassador, I share the title with a hero of mine, the late, great Audrey Hepburn, who once said, 'As you grow older, you will discover you have two hands: one for helping others, and one for helping yourself.' And that's exactly what I intend to do. I am looking forward to travelling to see UNICEF's amazing work and meeting as many children as I can. I want to inspire my fans to come on this journey with me, to learn with me and to raise their voices with mine. Starting today, let's remind ourselves of our rights as children, and let's demand those rights – not just for ourselves, but for every child here. So on World Children's Day, please join me and thousands of children around the world in taking actions for children today.

Bana Alabed

EDUCATION AND HUMAN RIGHTS ADVOCATE, SYRIAN REFUGEE

Bana Alabed is a young survivor of the Syrian Civil War, a conflict that has killed civilians, uprooted families, and caused fear and instability throughout the region. She garnered public attention around the world through a Twitter account she maintained through the 2016 bombing and siege of the city of Aleppo; the horrors of war gained special poignancy when communicated through the eyes of a seven-year-old girl.

After her school was destroyed and her father was injured in the siege, her family joined other civilians in fleeing the war-torn city; ultimately seeking refuge in Turkey. With the assistance of her mother, Fatemah, a former secondary school English teacher, Bana continues to tweet to over 300,000 followers, promoting peace and access to education, occasionally delivering speeches – such as the one at the IDA Awards in 2018 – and responding to questions from journalists in television interviews to further raise awareness about the crisis in Syria.

Speech at International Documentary Association (IDA) Awards

Los Angeles, California, USA · 2018

It is my pleasure to meet you.

… I would like to thank you for helping the Syrian children … I am lucky because I am alive, but I am sad because Syrian children [are] dying every day. They are suffering because there is no food or medicine. They can't go to school. We are children. We don't know what is the war. We need peace. We need a safe place to live in. The children should go to school, learn, feel happy.

… One day, we were learning at a school, and we heard the warplanes in the sky. My mum and my teacher decided to go home because it is dangerous. But we feel sad that we will go. It is the only time because the bombs [were] so dangerous … And then we hear the big bomb, we feel scared and run to home. When we arrive at home, we go to the basement. And then my dad [came] and told us that my school [was] bombed. I feel so sad that I will not see my friends again or learn. Please, stand together for peace and to stop the war. Thank you.

Greta Thunberg

ENVIRONMENTAL ACTIVIST

To make change in the world, sometimes you have to play by the rules. Other times, it's worth overturning the whole board and calling out an unfair game. Swedish student Greta Thunberg's take-no-prisoners attitude is exemplified in her speeches, implicating powerful politicians and the capitalist economic system in the degradation of our earth's climate. At the World Economic Forum in Davos, an annual gathering famous for its rich and famous attendees, she spoke about climate change and told her elite audience, 'Our house is on fire ... I want you to panic. I want you to feel the fear I feel every day. We owe it to the young people, to give them hope.'

Greta's journey began in an unlikely place. In August 2018, she skipped school and sat down in front of the Swedish parliament building with a hand-painted sign declaring a school strike by students around the world if world leaders did not take decisive action on climate change. In November 2018, her message gained traction, with more students joining and others filming her call to action on social media. By December that year, more than 20,000 students around the world across 270 towns and cities in countries across the world (including the UK, US, Japan and Belgium)

had joined her in striking and pressuring their governments to comply with the Paris Agreement.

Before Greta started her School Strike for Climate, her parents expressed concern about the pressures that activism would bring down on her shoulders. Their worry was understandable. Greta is on the autism spectrum and has selective mutism, which meant that she had a harder time with social situations than many of her peers. Few roles are more public than that of the activist, who is called upon to travel to conferences, deliver speeches, and meet with leaders, all while flashing a charismatic smile. But Greta is redefining what an activist looks like. By resisting the impulse to compromise or cushion her language, simply telling the truth with all the vigour and urgency the reality of climate change requires, she is showing that she is speaking up for the young generation and the health of the Earth, not to be popular.

In December 2018, she addressed the United Nations Climate Change Conference in Katowice, Poland, with a thundering condemnation of adults' lackadaisical responses to climate change in the status quo.

You say you love your children above all else, and yet you are stealing their future in front of their very eyes.

———————

Greta Thunberg

Age 15

Speech at COP24

Katowice, Poland · 2018

My name is Greta Thunberg. I am fifteen years old and I am from Sweden. I speak on behalf of Climate Justice Now. Many people say that Sweden is just a small country and it doesn't matter what we do. But I've learned that you are never too small to make a difference. And if a few children can get headlines all over the world just by not going to school, then imagine what we could all do together if we really wanted to.

... But to do that, we have to speak clearly, no matter how uncomfortable that may be. You only speak of green eternal economic growth because you are too scared of being unpopular. You only talk about moving forward with the same bad ideas that got us into this mess, even when the only sensible thing to do is pull the emergency brake. You are not mature enough to tell it like it is. Even that burden you leave to us children. But I don't care about being popular. I care about climate justice and the living planet. Our civilisation is being sacrificed for the opportunity of a very small number of people to continue making enormous amounts of money. Our biosphere is being sacrificed so that rich people in countries like mine can live in luxury. It is the sufferings of the many which pay for the luxuries of the few.

... The year 2078, I will celebrate my seventy-fifth birthday. If I have children maybe they will spend that day with me. Maybe they will ask me about you. Maybe they will ask why you didn't do anything while there still was time to act. You say you love your children above all else, and yet you are stealing their future in front of their very eyes.

... Until you start focusing on what needs to be done rather than what is politically possible, there is no hope. We cannot solve a crisis without treating it as a crisis. We need to keep the fossil fuels in the ground, and we need to focus on equity. And if solutions within the system are so impossible to find, maybe we should change the system itself. We have not come here to beg world leaders to care. You have ignored us in the past and you will ignore us again. We have run out of excuses and we are running out of time. We have come here to let you know that change is coming, whether you like it or not. The real power belongs to the people.

Canwen Xu

ADVOCATE FOR ASIAN-AMERICAN HERITAGE

Canwen Xu was born in Nanjing, China, and moved to the United States at the age of two. Just under 6 per cent of the United States population self-identifies as being of Asian descent, and there are certain regions that are noticeably lacking in minority groups. Canwen's childhood was spent moving around such places, as she lived in some of the least racially diverse states in the Midwest region of the country. These experiences made her finely attuned to the challenges of being a minority in primarily white spaces, as well as the ways in which Asian-Americans occupy a unique space in American social fabric. Canwen's experience of not fitting in and constantly receiving reminders from even well-meaning people that she did not look like her peers affected her deeply as she grew up. Although she experienced many moments that made her feel othered and ashamed of her Chinese heritage while growing up, she ultimately concludes, 'I am proud of who I am. A little bit American, a little bit Chinese, and a whole lot of both.'

In high school, Canwen was the National Membership Director and Idaho State Director for the Young Democrats High School Caucus. Also a programmer, she started an all-girls' computer science workshop called Code For Fun and received National Runner-Up in the 2014 NCWIT Aspirations in Computing competition. She is a student at Columbia University in New York and a passionate advocate of Asian-American issues. She spoke to an audience of fellow Midwest-dwelling Asian-American students about asserting Asian identity in America and being able to disentangle your feelings over the treatment you receive for being a minority from your feelings about your heritage itself.

Embrace your identity, embrace your contradiction, and most importantly, be bold while doing it.

Canwen Xu

Age 21

Midwest Asian-American Student Union Speech

University of Colorado Boulder, Colorado, USA · 2019

A couple months ago I was home for winter break in Boise, Idaho and I biked to a nearby salon to get my eyebrows done ... The esthetician was a friendly blonde woman who also lived in the neighborhood. We began to have a conversation ... After a while, she asked – where are you from? ...

I'm sure many of you have heard of the term, 'perpetual foreigner syndrome'... It essentially means that no matter how assimilated Asian-Americans may be, we are still treated like we're not from here ... This country is the only one that I've ever really known. However, it seems that even when Asian-Americans are completely Americanized, even if their family has lived in the States for generations, they are still seen as the other ...

[Growing up], the desire to recognize my own Asianness manifested itself only in private ... YouTube, for many of us, was the Asian Hollywood we never had. Before the existence of *Crazy Rich Asians*, or *Fresh Off the Boat*, YouTube was the place where we could live and breathe the Asian-American experience. It was a place where I was the norm, where I didn't feel like a contradiction anymore.

Watching these videos made me realize that I don't have to pick one identity or the other. I don't have to change myself into a person who finds mainstream depictions of a quote-unquote 'normal person' relatable. I don't have to whitewash my experiences, my outlook, my personality.

... Despite the unique experiences that Asian-Americans face, we are often left out of the race conversation. Asian-Americans are often placed in a grey zone. I myself said this in my speech three years ago. But since then, I've changed my mind ... I know in my heart that as Asian-Americans we are not grey. We are bold ... Even if we become white-washed, we will never be white ...

The question of 'where are you from?' used to bother me on two different levels. The first level, as I described earlier, was that I felt perpetually foreign ... The second level, which I don't like talking about, was that I didn't feel proud to be from China ... After all, it was this characteristic of being Chinese that had alienated me throughout my life from so many of the people around me. I admit, to this day, I am still trying to disassociate the otherness imposed upon me because of this identity from the identity itself. Because the issue was never that I hated being Chinese—the issue was that I hated the way I was treated because I was Chinese. And somehow, in the midst of living in both the Dakotas and Idaho, these two were conflated, and I began to resent my own identity.

... So my hope is that this community will give you what Columbia's Asian-American community has given to me, which is a sense of pride in yourself and your identity... Embrace your identity, embrace your contradiction, and most importantly, be bold while doing it.

Maya S. Penn

PHILANTHROPIST, ENVIRONMENTAL ACTIVIST, ENTREPRENEUR, ANIMATOR AND CEO

Maya S. Penn wears many hats: she is the CEO of her own clothing company as well as an animator, filmmaker, writer, author and activist.

Her work began at the age of eight, when she came up with the idea for her sustainable fashion brand, Maya's Ideas. She worked tirelessly to build the company from the ground up, including designing a website from scratch and shipping products to customers around the world. The success of her business garnered media attention and countless public speaking invitations, including one from the prestigious TEDWomen conference in 2013. Her address there received over 1.6 million views and counting globally. In 2016, she published a book, entitled *You Got This! Unleash Your Awesomeness, Find Your Path, and Change the World*, to help other young people discover their passions.

Maya's entrepreneurship has always been closely interwoven with a desire to promote social good. In a time when the fashion industry is increasingly under fire for contributing to the climate crisis through depleting natural resources and polluting the environment, Maya advocates sustainable design. She writes on her website,

'I do not use new wool, leather, silk, coral, etc. in my designs. If I come across a piece of 1940s vintage wool, silk, etc., fabric, I will use it and turn it into a brand-new creation. I always use old, vintage fabrics or organic bio-based materials like cotton. I use 100 per cent organic cotton, hemp, and bamboo, as well as recycled vintage materials in creating my clothing and accessories.'

Maya also donates a percentage of her profits to non-profit organizations working on environmental issues and women's rights, and launched a spinoff non-profit called Maya's Ideas 4 the Planet to help provide funding to up-and-coming female entrepreneurs. Moreover, she is the producer of an animated environmental series, *The Pollinators*.

In 2019 the US-based tween fashion brand Justice invited Maya to deliver the keynote address at its Live Justice Summit for young women. Maya, then nineteen years old, shared her story with other youth and encouraged them to speak up about their own ideas – even in the face of self-doubt or external criticism.

Even though I didn't have a lot to start with, I had a vision, and I was going to make it work.

———

Maya Penn

Age 19

Keynote Speaker at Live Justice Summit 2019

Columbus, Ohio, USA • 2019

I started my company, Maya's Ideas, in 2008. I was only eight years old when I started. My business really came from a mix of three things: my curiosity ... my love for the environment ... and my love for art and design in all its forms ... I knew that when I started my business, I was serious about it ... This wasn't going to be one of my pretend restaurants in my bedroom selling plastic pizzas to my stuffed animals ... This was going to be a real business, and it was going to be awesome ...

I started out making headbands, using whatever I had around the house ... Even though I didn't have a lot to start with, I had a vision, and I was going to make it work ... As I continued, I learned how to make new items, like hats and scarves and bags. I also knew that ... I wanted to give 10 per cent of my profits to local and global charities and environmental and women's rights organizations, because I know how important giving back is ...

Not only did I create my own products, I made my own logo. I was customer service and I researched branding and marketing ... I got into coding and taught myself HTML when I was ten to build my own official website. There was literally no hat I would not wear; I mean that metaphorically and literally ...

As I continued to grow and started selling my items online, my items started selling all over the world, to Italy and Denmark and Australia and Japan ... *Forbes* magazine reached out to me when I was ten years old. They wanted to feature me and my business in their magazine ... I started getting featured in TV shows and magazines ... I was blown away; I couldn't believe that this one idea I had at eight years old started snowballing into all these different opportunities for me. It shows how important it is to listen to all your ideas, big or small. You might have an idea cross your mind and you might subconsciously shoo it away ... but don't. Listen to your thoughts ...

The most successful public speakers all get nervous ... Taking on the world while not knowing if you can take on the world—that to me is true confidence ... You have to be friends with your feelings. You can't let your feelings drive the car, you've got to put those nerves in the backseat ... but you can still coexist with them and kick butt and be successful. You can still do it; take it from me. I do lots of public speaking, and I still get nervous, but I'm a professional, and it's important to remember your voice is important ...

[Critics] might try to stop you ... but they can never take your joy ... even when things get scary or things get tough—they can never steal your joy, because it's yours to keep ... If you keep moving and staying motivated, that's what matters in the end. I want you guys to repeat after me: I am strong. I am smart. I am awesome. I am beautiful inside and out. I can achieve anything I set my mind to. I will always go for my goals. I will lift up and support other girls. And I know other girls will lift up and support me. I got this. We got this!

Hilde Lysiak

JOURNALIST

At just twelve years old, Hilde Lysiak broke news stories about murders and drug deals at a speed many adult reporters would envy. Hilde is the youngest member of the Society for Professional Journalists, and the founder, publisher and sole reporter at *Orange Street News*, a local print and online news outlet dedicated to breaking news in the town of Selinsgrove, Pennsylvania. The daughter of a former reporter for the *New York Daily News*, Hilde grew up seeing the excitement of reporting first-hand when her father would take her to visit the newsroom. Although the first edition of the *Orange Street News* was simple – a newspaper for her family, written out in crayon – it quickly grew beyond the original scope of the project when Hilde found out about a homicide near her home and, undaunted, covered it before any other journalists in the area.

Orange Street News now has over one million online hits, and people around the world have paid attention to Hilde's journalism. However, her reporting has not just earned her friends, it has also earned her the scepticism (or outright hostility) of some local power players, including one police officer who told her she could be 'thrown in juvie' (juvenile detention) when he was disgruntled about her filming him as she sought to get an answer to a question.

In her commencement speech to the graduates of West Virginia University's Reed School of Media, Hilde advised her audience to never forget they serve the people rather than powerful individuals or governments, and expressed optimism about how a new generation of reporters, by sticking to tried-and-tested fundamentals of reporting such as objectivity and being embedded in local communities, could usher in an era of renewed trust in journalism.

We are the generation that can restore the people's trust. That is a trust I guard with my life. You should too.

Hilde Lysiak

Age 12

Commencement Speech to the Reed School of Media

West Virginia University, Morgantown, USA · 2019

Everywhere we turn we see bad news about the news, like how people don't buy newspapers anymore ... A week doesn't go by where someone doesn't tell me I should find another job. You know, one with a future. And I'm only twelve ...

Look, there is another path. But getting there won't be easy. As someone who has written hundreds of stories, exposed countless cases of corruption and developed a devoted readership that spans all across the world, I have some ideas on how we can create a bridge to *that* future ...

Talk to real people ... My best stories never came from a press release—they came from biking down my main street, knocking on doors, and talking to ... small business owners. That group of old people who hang out at the coffee shop. Or just the nice neighbor man who is raking leaves. It is here, buried in the nosey lady next door or at the church dinner, where the real nuggets of gold can be found. Real people have real stories ...

Trust no one ... Sometimes cops lie. Sometimes government officials lie. And yes, sometimes even the everyday people lie. That's why it is important to have your loyalty *not* to any personalities but to the truth ...

Get away from your desk ... The best reporters I know aren't waiting for the story to hit their inbox. They go find the story. As publisher, editor and the only reporter of the *Orange Street News*, I don't have an assignment editor. I have to generate my own story ideas. That is why after waking up every day at 4.30 in the morning the first thing I do is to go outside and run a mile. I also try to be part of my community. I go to the local restaurants and shop at the local stores. I'm out there ... I promise, the more time you spend exploring the world around you, the more the stories will find you ...

Everybody wants to change the world. And a reporter is armed with the most persuasive tool in the world—the facts. That is why a fair reporter can inspire far more change than even the best opinion columnist in the world ... Readers are smart. More often than not when given the right facts they will come to the right conclusions. That's the power of the truth ...

There is a crisis in media ... The crisis we are facing is one of trust ... Too many people just don't trust what they are reading anymore ... Too many of today's reporters made a decision to start mixing their reporting with a kind of theatre, a disgusting sort of political-based entertainment that seeks to divide people along political party lines to fulfill whatever bias they might feel or maybe to generate page clicks ...

We are the generation that can restore the people's trust ... That is a trust I guard with my life. You should too. As you move forward, it will be your most important currency ...

I believe history will look back on this moment not as the dark last days before the profession of journalism died, but as a new beginning when this generation ... didn't just save the news, but ushered in a new golden age of fact-based information that shined a light so bright it touched every corner of the globe.

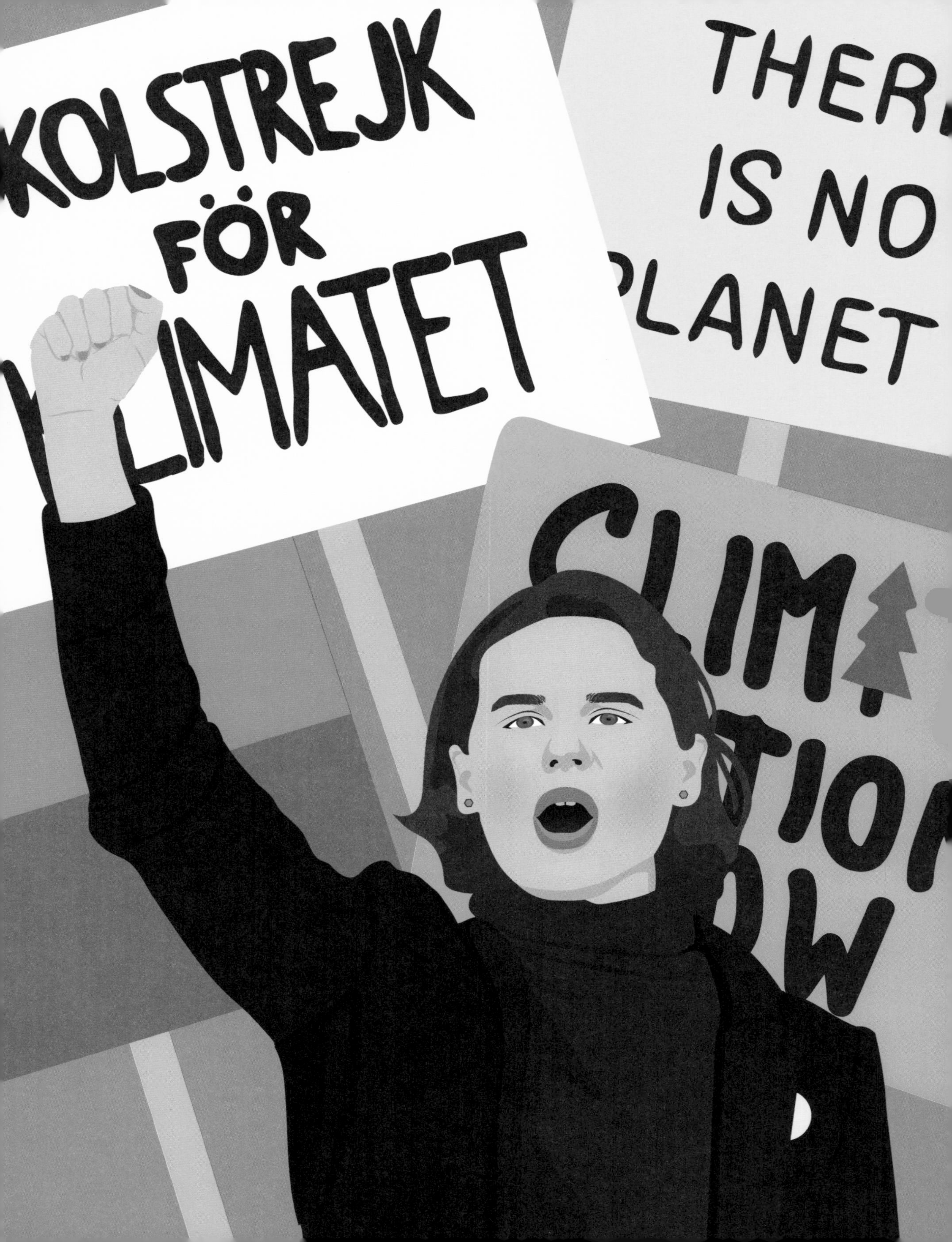
KOLSTREJK
FÖR
LIMATET
THER
IS NO
LANET
CLIM
TION
OW

Anuna De Wever

CLIMATE CHANGE ACTIVIST

Belgian climate activist Anuna De Wever's passion for environmental activism began with an early awareness of gender issues. She said in an interview with *Buzzfeed News* that early experiences with questioning gender identity (identifying as a boy in primary school, later switching to a more fluid self-identification and preferring female pronouns) made her willing to question conventional adult wisdom about how the world works. Later, attending a United Nations Commission on the Status of Women conference in 2016, she learned that the effects of climate change and natural disasters fell more destructively on the shoulders of women. When her mother suggested she watch a speech by climate activist Greta Thunberg, Anuna was inspired to get involved in the climate struggle herself, going on to lead the Youth for Climate movement in Belgium. She has delivered speeches around the world, worked with other youth climate activists and helped organize fellow students participating in the global School Strike for Climate.

At a Youth for Climate demonstration in Antwerp covered by the *De Morgen* newspaper, she declared, 'For far too long, politicians and rulers have got away with not doing anything to combat the climate crisis. We will ensure that they will not get away with it. We [engage in] truancy because we have done our homework and they have not. We do not fight for our future, but for everyone's future and we will not stop.' That Antwerp demonstration was attended by over 35,000 people. These demonstrations have received attention from media and politicians, not always positive. Reacting to striking students, the Flanders environment minister Joke Schauvliege said that the truants were a 'set-up', implying that some kind of broader conspiracy was behind the youth activism, later resigning over the comments.

Anuna responds to blatant cynicism from adults with a clear sense of determination and persistence. Along with her former Youth for Climate co-director, Kyra Gantois, Anuna received the 69th Ark Prize of the Free World from the German Marshall Fund of the United States. She addressed an audience of politicians at the Brussels Forum in summer 2019, highlighting how little had been accomplished politically and how much remained to be done.

I'm asking you: please be the first, be the ones that make the brave decisions.

Anuna de Wever

Age 18

Youth Activism and Climate

Brussels Forum, Belgium · 2019

I'm a climate activist from Belgium, and I have been for a very long time. When I was seven years old, I was in primary school and with the whole school we went to the city hall to sing for the climate. The song went like this: 'We need to wake up, we need to rise up, we need to open our eyes and ... build a better future and we need to start right now.'

... I'm eighteen years old today. It's been eleven years, and nothing has happened. It has only gotten worse ... The climate crisis is not something that is far away; it is happening right now. We have children in Mozambique who have seen their homes flooded by the rising sea level and their cities destroyed by hurricanes, the millions of animal species that die every year because of climate change, and people that die every year because of climate change. But still we don't see a change of habits. We have to be honest with ourselves: we are living in a fossil fuel-addicted society. But still, it is so easy for us for some reason to just get back into our comfort zone, close our eyes to the problem, and run away from the danger that is facing us ...

We have to act right now. Climate change has not been a priority, and we have had a mentality of the 'sky's the limit' and economic growth without thinking about the consequences for this planet Earth. But lots of economists have already said that economic growth can go hand in hand with actually taking care of this planet ...

We have had strikes in more than 130 countries with people coming on the streets every week demanding political action and climate justice. But we can only dream of change. And I know there are people in this room who have the power to make that change ... So I'm asking you: please be the first, be the ones that make the brave decisions. I know that sometimes it sounds impossible, how do you solve an existential crisis, right? But humanity has already shown how much it can do. We made a whole world run on technology in a decade. We ended not one, but two, world wars ... We put a man on the moon.

... 195 countries signed the Paris Agreement, and not one of them is in line with the targets that they have set. If we're not in line with the targets in the Paris Agreement ... we will reach a tipping point and the earth will warm itself up, climate change will be irreversible, and I won't have a future anymore. So the first step is the hardest. The first step is you leaving this room after my talk knowing you will also have to be part of the revolution ... to join in the fight for our future.

More Young People to Inspire

There are too many excellent youth speakers to be able to include every single one in this anthology, but I hope you see *Speak Up!* as a starting point for further research and discovery. Around the world, so many young people are using their voices to call for change, sometimes risking their reputations, their careers and their lives. Unlike written articles that are published in print or online, speeches can be uniquely ephemeral. We don't know exactly how many rabble-rousing orations shouted into megaphones at rallies may have been lost to time, but we do know that there is a significant disparity in those whose voices have been considered worth recording in history. In some situations, while researching for this book, I found that there were insufficient archival materials (transcripts or recordings of speeches) to include someone. In other situations, language barriers may have been at play. However, whether or not someone's speeches have been recorded in a language you understand, I think their work can inspire you to take on challenges in your own community. Here are some more inspiring young people:

Claudette Colvin

Months before Rosa Parks became famous for the same act of civil disobedience, a fifteen-year-old girl named Claudette Colvin refused to give up her seat on a segregated city bus in Montgomery, Alabama, and was arrested by white police officers in 1955. She became a plaintiff in *Browder v. Gayle*, a United States District Court case that ruled on Alabama bus segregation laws.

Iqbal Masih

At just four years old, Iqbal became a debt slave, forced to work long hours in a carpet factory in Pakistan to help pay off a loan for his mother's medical care. At the age of ten, he escaped the factory's torturous conditions and started school with the help of an NGO, the Bonded Labour Liberation Front. He quickly became an activist, delivering speeches around the world to speak out against child labour. He was fatally shot in 1995, but his life and work inspired the United States Congress to establish an annual award for anti-child labour activism, human rights advocates Marc and Craig Kielburger to found the charity Free the Children, and the building of schools around the world.

Emma González

When Emma was a fourth-year high school student at Marjory Stoneman Douglas High School in Parkland, Florida, a gunman opened fire and killed seventeen of her classmates, injuring many more. In the aftermath of the shooting, Emma joined forces with several other students to speak out against gun violence and organize the 2018 demonstration against gun violence 'March for Our Lives', attended by over 1 million people – one of the largest demonstrations in US history.

Naomi Wadler

Naomi speaks out against gun violence in the United States, particularly drawing attention to the daily victims of gun crime – disproportionately black women – who are too often excluded from media narratives that focus on mass school shootings. Naomi delivered a speech about this at the 2018 'March for Our Lives' rally, where she was the youngest speaker.

Noma Nazir Bhatt, Farah Hassan, and Aneeqa Khalid

Indian teenagers Noma, Farah and Aneeqa formed the all-girl rock band Pragaash, which means 'first light' or 'from darkness to light' in Kashmiri. They garnered attention after their first public performance in December 2012, but also received a deluge of hateful comments and death threats. The girls faced condemnation from the Muslim-majority state's Grand Mufti (clerical leader), who said women performing music in public was un-Islamic. Safety concerns forced the girls to stop playing, but not before their bravery elicited support from India and around the world.

Yara Shahidi

Yara Shahidi is an American actress and activist who uses her platform to raise awareness about numerous social justice issues, including representation and diversity in media and youth voting. When she turned eighteen, she hosted a voter registration party and kickstarted the 'Eighteen x 18' campaign intended to increase voting turnout.

Joshua Wong

Joshua is a pro-democracy activist in Hong Kong who has been jailed several times for his outspoken opposition to the central Chinese government. In 2011, at the age of fourteen, he created a student-led political group called Scholarism. Three years later, he organized a school boycott and took part in a massive occupation known as the Umbrella Movement, involving thousands of students and other demonstrators blocking major roadways for seventy-nine days as they called for free elections.

• Emma González •

• Naomi Wadler •

Mari Copeny

Mari, known as 'Little Miss Flint', hails from the American city of Flint, Michigan, where polluted drinking water exposed tens of thousands of people to elevated lead levels and dangerous bacteria – killing twelve people who contracted Legionnaire's Disease as a result. At just eight years old, Mari wrote a letter to President Obama asking him to visit Flint and help solve the situation. He later met with her and authorized $100 million in funding.

Rosie King

Rosie, a university student from Wakefield, UK, was diagnosed with Asperger's Syndrome at the age of nine. Her two younger siblings are also on the autism spectrum, and she wanted to increase public understanding of people with autism. She hosted a television programme for the BBC called 'My Autism and Me', earning her an Emmy Kids Award and worldwide recognition that led to a speaking invitation at the TED MED conference. Her speech has received over 2.6 million views.

Netiwit Chotiphatphaisal

Netiwit is a Thai student activist. In 2012, at the age of sixteen, he worked with fellow students to form the Thai Education Revolution Alliance, advocating for increasing the quality of public education and decreasing the emphasis on old-fashioned, rote-style memorization in learning. Netiwit's pro-democracy activism has earned him high-powered enemies, and he has been detained for protesting against the military government. But he has also earned notable supporters, like the eight Nobel laureates who sent a letter to his university after it placed sanctions on him for his advocacy.

Frank Waln

Frankis an indigenous Sicangu Lakota American rapper, songwriter and activist. In 2010, at the age of twenty-one, he formed the musical group Nake Nula Waun, releasing an album that same year. Frank uses hip-hop music to tell the story of oppression, genocide and trauma faced by Native Americans, hoping to combat stereotypes and the invisibility of indigenous people in American popular culture.

· Rosie King ·

· Frank Waln ·

Adut Akech

Adut is a South Sudanese-Australian model who began modelling at sixteen years old. She lived in a refugee camp in Kenya until the age of eight, when her family moved to Australia. At school, she faced bullying from classmates over the colour of her skin, but didn't allow the cruel words to damage her own sense of beauty. As a highly successful model, Adut has spoken openly about her own struggles with mental health, destigmatizing a sometimes challenging subject; she has also stood up for diversity in the fashion industry.

Amanda Nguyen

Amanda is an American activist and the founder and CEO of Rise, an organization that advocates for the rights of survivors of sexual assault. Amanda is herself a survivor, and realized she faced a daunting system of bureaucratic hoops if she wanted to press charges. The traumatic experience led Amanda to work on drafting a bill to protect the rights of sexual assault survivors, including ensuring that rape kits would be preserved at no charge for the length of the statute of limitations for pressing charges. The bill passed through the US Congress unanimously and was signed into law in October 2016. Since 2016, Rise has helped pass more than twenty laws.

Babar Ali

Babar has been called 'the youngest headmaster in the world'. He was only nine years old when he saw children his own age in his hometown of Murshidabad, India, picking garbage instead of going to school. Determined to change things, he founded a school in his own backyard, teaching the children how to read. In 2015, with support from the local community, the school, called Ananda Siksha Niketan, moved from Babar's backyard to a nearby building. Babar has educated more than 5,000 children, and advocates throughout India for increased access to education.

Talia Leman

At the age of ten, Talia saw the damage and chaos wreaked by Hurricane Katrina in Louisiana, USA, and raised over $10 million for the natural disaster's victims by motivating millions of children around the world to donate. She then founded a non-profit organization called RandomKid, intended to help provide an umbrella organization for the charity endeavours of other youth who might otherwise not be able to receive and disperse funds.

• Babar Ali •

• Amandla Stenberg •

Thandiwe Abdullah

Thandiwe founded the Black Lives Matter Youth Vanguard, an advocacy group that fights excessive policing in public schools and advocates for the rights of black youth. She spoke in front of 500,000 people at the 2018 Women's March in Los Angeles. In February 2019, as a fifteen-year-old sophomore in high school, she was honoured by the Los Angeles City Council in recognition of her work.

Amandla Stenberg

Amandla Stenberg is an American actress and singer who has been outspoken on issues of race, gender, and sexuality. At the age of sixteen, she publicly shared a video she initially made for a history class project called 'Don't Cash Crop My Cornrows' about cultural appropriation and black culture. She has also spoken about hoping to provide representation to other black girls and discusses being a member of the LGBTQ+ community, saying in a video for *Teen Vogue*, 'I believe in the concept of rebellion through selfhood.'

Amani Al-Khatahtbeh

Amani is an American writer and entrepreneur who founded the website MuslimGirl.com, a popular women's blog by and for Muslim women, at the age of seventeen. She is passionate about creating community and amplifying the voices of Muslim women and youth, especially in a political environment of widespread Islamophobia.

Jasilyn Charger

Jasilyn Charger is a Native American environmental activist, water protector, and member of the Cheyenne River Sioux Tribe. She launched the International Indigenous Youth Council at the age of twenty-one, catalysed by the threat posed to her people by the proposed Dakota Access Pipeline. In protest against the pipeline construction, Jasilyn organized a 2,000-mile run from North Dakota to the capital of Washington, D.C.

Sixto Cancel

Sixto is an American non-profit leader and advocate for foster care reform. He founded the organization Think of Us to advocate and provide resources for youth in – or about to exit – the foster care system. Sixto and his team also co-organized and executed the first White House Foster Care and Technology Hackathon.

Adiba Khan

Adiba is an American advocate for reproductive justice. While attending college at the University of California, Berkeley, she became the founder and director of Students United for Reproductive Justice (SURJ), the university's first undergraduate pro-choice organization. With SURJ, Adiba helped campaign for a California bill requiring the state's public universities to offer medication abortion services at college student health centres, rather than forcing students in need of this medical procedure to go to hospitals or clinics off-campus. Both of the state's legislative houses ultimately passed the bill.

Zulaikha Patel

At the age of thirteen, South African student Zulaikha became the face of a movement against rules at her Pretoria high school that prohibited young women from wearing afros and other natural hairstyles. A video showing her and fellow students engaged in a tense standoff with security forces went viral, and the movement took off on social media, provoking broader conversations about racism in education in post-apartheid South Africa. The school amended its rules and Zulaikha remains active as a fighter against racism and sexism.

Read All About It!

From hands-on advice for young people to a more philosophical exploration of how education works in our society, the books below provide guidance and provocation that may be helpful to anyone interested in speaking up.

A Random Book about the Power of ANYone
Talia Leman
(Simon and Schuster)

It's Your World: Get Informed, Get Inspired & Get Going!
Chelsea Clinton
(Penguin Random House)

Freedom's Orator: Mario Savio and the Radical Legacy of the 1960s
Robert Cohen
(Oxford University Press)

I Am Malala
Malala Yousafzai
(Little, Brown and Company)

Under the Same Sky: From Starvation in North Korea to Salvation in America
Joseph Kim
(Houghton Mifflin Harcourt)

So Here I Am: Speeches by Great Women to Empower and Inspire
Anna Russell
(White Lion Publishing)

The Opposite of Loneliness: Essays and Stories
Marina Keegan
(Scribner)

Pedagogy of the Oppressed
Paulo Freire
(Continuum)

Credits

Joan of Arc

Mario Savio

Reprinted by permission of Lynne Hollander Savio.

Severn Cullis-Suzuki

Reprinted by permission of Severn Cullis-Suzuki.

Rhiannon Tomtishen & Madison Vorva

Used with permission of Bioneers.

Jack Andraka

Reprinted by permission of Jack Andraka.

Easton LaChappelle

Reprinted by permission of Easton LaChappelle, Unlimited Tomorrow and Business Innovation Factory.

Kelvin Doe

© DJ Focus.

Madison Kimrey

Reprinted with permission of Madison Kimrey.

Joseph Kim

Reprinted by permission of Joseph Kim.

Melissa Shang

Reprinted with permission of Melissa Shang's parent/legal guardian, Sue Liu.

Jazz Jennings

© I Am Jazz LLC.

Malala Yousafzai

Malala Yousafzai's Speech to the United Nations. Reproduced with permission of Curtis Brown Group Ltd, on behalf of Malala Yousafzai. Copyright © Malala Yousafzai, 2015.

Patrick Kane

Patrick T J Kane © 2015.

Emer Hickey & Ciara Judge

Reprinted by permission of Ciara Judge and Emer Hickey.

Raymond Wang

Reprinted by permission of Raymond Wang.

Megan Grassell

Reprinted by permission of Megan Grassell.

Kenneth Shinozuka

Reprinted by permission of Kenneth Shinozuka.

Tara Subramaniam

Reprinted by permission of Tara Subramaniam.

Joshua Browder

Reprinted by permission of Joshua Browder.

Krtin Nithiyanandam

Reprinted by permission of Krtin Nithiyanandam.

Ishita Katyal

Reprinted by permission of Ishita Katyal.

Acknowledgements

No book is a solo project. I am indebted to all the youth speakers whose speeches are at the heart of this book. Your words inspire, challenge and invigorate me to keep on demanding justice and not give up, even when it feels like the world is on fire.

I am deeply grateful to everyone at White Lion Publishing: Emma Harverson, Zara Anvari and Philippa Wilkinson for their exciting vision and stewardship of this book, Ramona Lamport for meticulous copyediting, and Bella Skertchly for invaluable research assistance. Coordinating a book over an ocean and multiple timezones is not easy, and I feel deeply lucky to have had the opportunity to work with such understanding editors.

I credit several groups and organizations for helping me to realize that giving young people greater opportunities for autonomy and activism is one of the crucial issues of our time. Through education conferences in the United States I met some peers passionate about amplifying student voice in education reform who would become dear friends. The ambition and thoughtfulness provoked late-night conversations (and debates) about what a better world for youth might look like.

This journey probably would not have begun without a speech I gave when I was twelve years old, and that speech would not have been possible without the faith of TED curator Chris Anderson and content director Kelly Stoetzel. I'm also grateful for numerous programs at TED that give opportunities to youth (TEDx and TED-Ed in particular), and the incredible team members of the TEDxRedmond conference who I worked with between 2010 and 2013. All of these people have great faith in the possibility for young people to shake the ground on which we stand and build a better future for all.

Perhaps no group better exemplifies that faith in the potential of young people than educators. My deep gratitude goes to my childhood teacher Felisa Rogers and everyone at Redmond High School and UC Berkeley who inspired me greatly.

Finally, I owe a massive debt of gratitude to my parents, John and Joyce Svitak, my sister Adrianna, and numerous friends who have provided social and emotional support, chiefly Arjun Dave. Love is at the heart of all great efforts for social change, and it is perhaps through my friends' acts of compassion that I have learned most directly about what it means to make the world a better place.